WRITERS AND CRITICS

Chief Editors
A. NORMAN JEFFARES
R. L. C. LORIMER

Advisory Editors
DAVID DAICHES   C. P. SNOW

D. H. LAWRENCE

ANTHONY BEAL

CAPRICORN BOOKS
NEW YORK

Published by arrangement with

OLIVER AND BOYD LTD
Tweeddale Court
Edinburgh 1

Copyright © Text and Bibliography
Anthony Beal

First published 1961

Reprinted 1964
Reprinted 1966
Reprinted 1968

CAPRICORN BOOKS EDITION 1972

SBN: 399-50264-5
Library of Congress Catalog Card Number:
72-81101

PRINTED IN THE UNITED STATES OF AMERICA

CONTENTS

ACKNOWLEDGMENTS

For permission to reproduce all quotations from D. H. Lawrence's works, acknowledgments are due to the Trustees of the late Mrs Frieda Lawrence's Estate, to Laurence Pollinger Ltd, and to William Heinemann Ltd.

For permission to quote from the works indicated, acknowledgments are also due to the following: Chatto and Windus Ltd (F. R. Leavis, *D. H. Lawrence: Novelist*); W. Heffer and Sons Ltd (F. R. Leavis, *D. H. Lawrence*); Southern Illinois University Press (*A D. H. Lawrence Miscellany*, ed. Harry T. Moore).

The photograph on the front cover is reproduced by permission of the Radio Times Hulton Picture Library.

A.B.

ABBREVIATED TITLES
BY WHICH LAWRENCE'S WORKS
ARE CITED IN REFERENCES

A.R.	=	*Aaron's Rod.*
K.	=	*Kangaroo.*
L.	=	*The Letters of D. H. Lawrence.*
L.C.L.	=	*Lady Chatterley's Lover.*
L.G.	=	*The Lost Girl.*
P.	=	*Phoenix.*
P.S.	=	*The Plumed Serpent.*
R.	=	*The Rainbow.*
S.L.	=	*Sons and Lovers.*
S.L.C.	=	*Selected Literary Criticism.*
W.L.	=	*Women in Love.*
W.P.	=	*The White Peacock.*

CHAPTER I

THE EARLY NOVELS

"The difference between people isn't in their class, but in themselves. Only from the middle classes one gets ideas, and from the common people—life itself, warmth."[1] So speaks Paul Morel, the character who stands for Lawrence himself in *Sons and Lovers*, the autobiographical novel that tells so much about the first twenty-five years of his life, about his family and friends and the society in which he grew up. It is a story in which the warm, unthinking physical world of the common people (as typified by his father) is partly renounced for the "superior" life represented by his mother's aspirations towards middle-class education and ideas. And these two themes of "ideas" and "warm life" (with the same class connotations) were to remain important throughout Lawrence's life and work.

David Herbert Lawrence was born, the fourth child of a miner, on 11 September 1885, at Eastwood, some eight miles north-west of Nottingham. Coal had been mined in the district for centuries, but until about forty years before Lawrence's birth the process was still practically medieval. The miners lived in thatched cottages and worked their small mines in the hillsides, the coal being "drawn to the surface by donkeys that plodded wearily in a circle round a gin."[2] About 1850 the scene was transformed by the arrival of the capitalists and the railways. Large collieries were built amongst the fields; the old cottages gave way to decent but dull rows of brick dwellings built by the colliery companies; and rail-tracks enmeshed the previously unspoiled farmland, hills, and woods.

But it was still an extremely beautiful countryside, with the rich sandstone and oak-trees of Sherwood Forest to the east, and the more austere limestone hills of Derbyshire to the north-west. The mines were still, in a way, an accident in the landscape, and Eastwood itself remained a village rather than a town. It stood in a fine position on a hill-top and most of the houses looked out over open country. The miners walked through the fields to work, and on their way they might search for mushrooms in the long grass or pick up a stray rabbit for supper, like any other countrymen. So although the population of Eastwood could be classified as almost entirely "industrial working-class," it was a world far removed from the dense warrens of Victorian working-class London or Sheffield or Liverpool, and its inhabitants were emphatically not the submerged proletariat of the urban slums. They were manual workers who took pride in their work; and there seems to have been little threat of unemployment. Lawrence's father as a young man could earn up to £5 in a good week, at a time when rent cost only five or six shillings. (Some twenty years later, Lawrence, as a qualified teacher in London, earned less than £2 a week—and this was considered an exceptionally high salary.)

According to Lawrence, the miners themselves did not care very profoundly about their wages. They lived an almost purely instinctive life, developing a great sense of intimacy and comradeship with one another as they worked half-naked down the pit, and continuing this intimacy as they drank together in the pub after work. They were not at home in the daylight world of hard facts, of money and home responsibilities. But the colliers' wives had to live in this daylight world; they had to worry about the material things, and do their best to make decent, civilised homes for themselves and their children. And the closer the wives got to their desired middle-class standard of living, the more their collier-husbands appeared to them as blundering intruders from an alien, more primitive world.

It was this conflict between Lawrence's own parents that had a decisive effect on his life. His father was almost illiterate, while his mother was a woman of some education and refinement, determined that her sons should better themselves. But for her, Lawrence might never have acquired the education that enabled him to become a writer—and however much in later life he spoke against education and "mental life," no one can become a great novelist without them. No amount of physical, instinctive life alone can produce novels. Yet without his father's gift of "life itself, warmth," his mother's influence might have resulted in his becoming merely "a bright young prig" (as he once described himself). As a young man, Lawrence saw things very much with his mother's eyes, but the longer he lived the more he came to sympathise with his father. In his first novel, *The White Peacock*, he is closest to his mother's world; in his last, *Lady Chatterley's Lover*, the most remote from it.

Lawrence's novels are not only his spiritual autobiography. They also record in detail the actual physical surroundings and events of his life, and there are very few of his friends (or even acquaintances) who do not appear in his fiction in one form or another. Not unnaturally, many of these people published their reminiscences and impressions of Lawrence after his death—but these books are inevitably about the man himself. From some of them one would hardly gather that Lawrence was a writer. There are at least half-a-dozen books of this kind for every one that sets out to study his work, and personal vendettas irrelevant to the understanding or enjoyment of his writing have bedevilled criticism of it. So it is important to stress at the outset that Lawrence was not just a wonderful man, or a difficult man, or at times perhaps almost a mad man; not just a preacher, or a prophet, or an advocate of social and sexual reform—but, above all, a great writer. Here we are concerned with his writing, and his life is important only as it is reflected in his work. But before discussing his first book, it would perhaps be appropriate to give Lawrence's own laconic sketch of the chief events of his life up to the start of his literary career.

I was a delicate pale brat with a snuffy nose, whom most people treated quite gently as just an ordinary delicate little lad. When I was twelve I got a county council scholarship, twelve pounds a year, and went to Nottingham High School.

After leaving school I was a clerk for three months, then had a very serious pneumonia illness, in my seventeenth year, that damaged my health for life.

A year later I became a school teacher, and after three years' savage teaching of collier lads I went to take the "normal" course in Nottingham University.

As I was glad to leave school, I was glad to leave college. It had meant mere disillusion, instead of the living contact of men. From college I went down to Croydon, near London, to teach in a new elementary school at a hundred pounds a year.

It was while I was at Croydon, when I was twenty-three, that the girl who had been the chief friend of my youth, and who was herself a school teacher in a mining village at home, copied out some of my poems, and without telling me, sent them to the *English Review*, which had just had a glorious rebirth under Ford Madox Hueffer.

Hueffer was most kind. He printed the poems, and asked me to come and see him. The girl had launched me, so easily, on my literary career, like a princess cutting a thread, launching a ship.[3]

Shortly afterwards Lawrence showed Hueffer the manuscript of *The White Peacock*, which he had been writing and re-writing for four years. Hueffer read it and told Lawrence, "It's got every fault that the English novel can have. But, you've got GENIUS." The book was published in both England and America in 1911, when Lawrence was twenty-five.

Few people today come to Lawrence first by way of *The White Peacock*. Those who do will get only hints of the power of the later books; yet, once read, it is not easily forgotten. One's first impression is of a talented young man, acutely observant of nature and delighting in it. He never tires of descriptions of flowers, trees, birds—though the reader may. The observation is genuine, but the expression can be stilted and over-fanciful. Primroses look "wistfully" and "yearn darkly for the sun," bracken "held out arms for me," oaks "saved us a grateful shade." The things have been seen vividly, but Lawrence's vision is sometimes lost in the straining after a literary style.

It is the countryside of his youth that he is describing, the hills and woods and fields around Eastwood, with the notable difference that the mines and ugly paraphernalia of industrialism are missing. It is a countryside seen by a countryman who passionately loves it but at the same time has no illusions about its darker aspects: land runs wild and unprofitable; rabbits devour the crops and rats invade the barns; cottages are squalid or deserted; animals and birds are preyed upon, trapped, and killed.

Having expunged the mines, and the miners, from the scene, Lawrence also shifts the main characters one social class up from his own. The story is told in the first person, and the narrator's circumstances could be described as the fulfilment of Lawrence's mother's aspirations: the young man is apparently of independent means, lives with his mother and sister in solid middle-class comfort, paints water-colours, and leads an exemplary life. It is a world of Edwardian leisure, of lying in deckchairs, ringing for the servants, and dressing for dinner.

This assumption of a bourgeois background has a deadening effect on the book; and although it is the only novel that Lawrence wrote in the first person, it is the one where the presence of Lawrence himself is least felt. The narrator, Cyril, is an insubstantial figure, little more than an observer, and there is an artificiality and stiltedness about the other middle-class characters. It is not just that some of the small talk has dated disastrously ("We had a giddy ripping time in Coll., didn't we?"); the artificiality extends to many of the important conversations in the book. For example, the love-making between the narrator's sister, Lettie, and the man she marries, Leslie, is carried on in an impossibly literary, even archaic, style, liberally sprinkled with quotations and mythological references. Nothing could be further from the love-talk of *Lady Chatterley's Lover*, and this contrast between Lawrence's first novel and his last effectively illustrates the difference between the cultivated world of ideas and "life itself, warmth."

But not all the people in the book are leisured and affected—indeed, the one really striking character, George Saxton, is an earthy farmer's son working his land in rhythm with the seasons. Between him and Cyril there is an almost passionate attachment, and the scene where the two men bathe together is the forerunner of a number of episodes in Lawrence's novels, where two men achieve a spiritual harmony through physical contact:

He saw I had forgotten to continue my rubbing, and laughing he took hold of me and began to rub me briskly, as if I were a child, or rather, a woman he loved and did not fear. I left myself quite limply in his hands, and, to get a better grip on me, he put his arm round me and pressed me against him, and the sweetness of the touch of our naked bodies one against the other was superb. It satisfied in some measure the vague, indecipherable yearning of my soul; and it was the same with him. When he had rubbed me all warm, he let me go, and we looked at each other with eyes of still laughter, and our love was perfect for a moment, more perfect than any love I have known since, either for man or woman.[4]

Yet even George is infected by the prevailing mental consciousness. He decides, for example, that he would like to marry Lettie as a result of studying a book of Aubrey Beardsley's drawings: "The more I look at these naked lines, the more I want her."[5] But he is too *gauche* and lacking in initiative—one might almost say too nice—for the rather hoity-toity Lettie, and loses her to the smooth and wealthy Leslie (who eventually becomes a Tory M.P.).

George, having proved inadequate in the middle-class world of ideas, courts and wins the plump, good-hearted, and quite uneducated Meg, from the Ram Inn. Their wedding-day is one of the most delightful things in Lawrence. It begins with George, dressed as if for the cattle-market, arriving to collect his best man, Cyril, who gives him four of his water-colours as a wedding present. The description of these pictures exemplifies the lyrical, elegiac mood so typical of this youthful book:

They were drawings among the waters and the fields of the mill, grey rain and twilight, morning with the sun pouring gold into the mist, and the suspense of a midsummer noon upon the pond. All the glamour of our yesterdays came over him like an intoxicant, and he quivered with the wonderful beauty of life that was weaving him into the large magic of the years.[6]

The mood quickly changes. The two men set off by dog-cart to collect Meg, who has not even been told that it is her wedding-day. She is surprised in the middle of cooking and carried off in the face of vehement opposition from her bedridden grandmother. The adventures that they have on their way to the registry office (such as rescuing a baby from a collapsed push-chair); the wedding luncheon in Nottingham (" 'We'll go,' he said, 'to an hotel.' His eyes dilated as he said it, and she shrank away with delighted fear. Neither of them had ever been to an hotel.'"[7]); the afternoon on the river and in the park; the evening at the opera "like giddy dukes"—the whole episode goes with a swing and naturalness that Lawrence never surpassed. It is Chaucerian in its freshness, humour, tenderness, and delight in human nature. These are qualities which Lawrence has sometimes been accused of lacking, but this chapter alone, "A New Start in Life," should prove how wrong such charges are.

Soon—and one is not surprised—Meg has twins:

Thus she was perfect. She handled the bonny, naked child with beauty of gentleness. . . . She drooped her head with the grace of a Madonna, and her movements were lovely, accurate and exquisite, like an old song perfectly sung. Her voice, playing and soothing round the curved limbs of the baby, was like water, soft as wine in the sun, running with delight.[8]

But already George is partly forgotten:

A woman is so ready to disclaim the body of a man's love; she yields him her own soft beauty with so much gentle patience and regret; she clings to his neck, to his head and his cheeks, fondling them for the soul's meaning that is there, and shrinking from his passionate limbs and his body. . . .

"Meg never found any pleasure in me as she does in the kids," said George bitterly.[9]

It is, indeed, an impression of swarms of children (Meg's home is only one of a number of vividly-depicted domestic interiors, crowded with children), and of the profuse and incessant activities of nature, that *The White Peacock* leaves with the reader. The human relations are not very thoroughly worked out. The only character in whom we are interested is George, and he has a sad fate.

Just as the good land turns sour, so George, the frank, physical man, degenerates into a hopeless drunkard, ruining himself, his wife, and the children. Indeed, parts of the last chapter read like a temperance tract, and in this one must suspect the influence of Lawrence's mother, for whom drink was a major evil and her own husband one of its victims. When we recall that the father in this book also died of drink, it is obvious that the theme came very readily to Lawrence's mind at this time. A few years later, it would have been forgotten, and emphasis would have been put instead on the contrast between the natural, healthy, productive farm life, such as George leads at the beginning of the book, and the artificial, sterile life of Lettie and Leslie.

The White Peacock is a young man's book—almost, indeed, a virginal book. Life has been vividly observed, but little has been actually experienced—or, if it has, the experience has not been digested. So the book consists really of a number of disconnected episodes with no underlying development.

It is characteristic that the episode of the white peacock itself is irrelevant to the action of the rest of the novel. This is the story of Annable, the gamekeeper—an odd example of the story-within-a-story such as one finds in the novels of Dickens or Scott. Annable had been to Cambridge, become a parson, gone as curate to a parish whose rector was an earl's son, been pursued by the rector's cousin, Lady Crystabel, and married her, only to find that she didn't want children and "began to go souly." He leaves her and the Church, and now lives in a poor cottage with a sluttish woman and a horde of children. "He was a man of one idea:—that all civilisation was the painted fungus of rottenness. He hated any sign of culture."[10] The white peacock appears momentarily in the deserted churchyard attached to the big house for which the gamekeeper works. It perches on the stone angel of a headstone, excretes, lifts up its head and yells. "That's the very soul of a lady," says the game-keeper, "the very, very soul . . . all vanity and screech and defilement."[11] The episode is interesting chiefly because it contains the seeds of the story of Mellors, the game-keeper in *Lady Chatterley's Lover*.

Though the narrator and his family have been shifted up the social scale, *The White Peacock* partly reflects Lawrence's own life at Eastwood when he was a student in his early twenties. In particular, the farm where George and his family live in the book is closely based on a real farm and family that played a vital part in Lawrence's youth. A letter he wrote when he was twenty-two gives some idea of the fullness and happiness and variety of this life, divided between the farm and his home:

> Tomorrow we shall be in the fields again, pulling and finishing the stacks . . . we shall have some fun; Wednesday we shall walk to Codnor Castle—we shall be out all day, returning to the Haggs (a farm, the home of my friends)—where, in the low parlour, I shall read Verlaine to the girls . . . and perhaps I'll read Whitman; we shall walk arm in arm through the woods home in the moonlight. Thursday we have a party at home, when we sing; we learn then our songs, our Schumann, Giordani, Schubert and the song classics; we shall play bridge and be jolly.[12]

When we remember that "at home" was a miner's cottage, we see how far Mrs Lawrence's insistence on her sons being educated enabled Lawrence to escape from the philistinism of most of Eastwood life. In those days, the route by which young men, and still more girls, of the working class most often escaped to the comparative freedom of the middle class was by becoming teachers. Nearly all Lawrence's friends of his own age were teachers, with opportunities to think, to read and exchange ideas, and to free themselves of the almost suffocating sense of large families crowded into small cottages that is so powerfully conveyed in *The White Peacock*. But in the attainment of middle-class intellectual freedom there lay the danger of losing the old physical intimacy of the common people.

In Lawrence's second book this is recognised. The theme of *The Trespasser* is failure of contact, lack of warmth, between people. After the great sprawl of *The White Peacock*, this book has a classical unity and conciseness which emphasise the tautness of the emotions involved. The main action concerns two people only and takes place over a period of five days in one place on the Isle of Wight.

It is the story of Siegmund, a violinist, thirty-eight years old and married for half of them, whose relationship with his wife is now dead. He leaves her and his children to go on holiday with Helena, a schoolteacher of twenty-six, to whom he has taught music.

This was one of the crises of his life. For years he had suppressed his soul, in a kind of mechanical despair doing his duty and enduring the rest. Then his soul had been softly enticed from its bondage. Now he was going to break free altogether, to have at least a few days purely for his own joy. This, to a man of his integrity, meant a breaking of bonds, a severing of blood-ties, a sort of new birth.[13]

This is to be, therefore, as always in Lawrence, no mere erotic escapade but a "translation of himself." Helena is a self-possessed young woman "calm and full of her own assurance." She has preceded Siegmund to Freshwater, and on the evening of his arrival the flaw in their relationship is struck. He is intensely moved, "a tense, vivid body of flesh without a mind." But Helena's desire is accomplished in a kiss: "She belonged to that class of 'dreaming women' with whom passion exhausts itself at the mouth":

He held her close. His dream was melted in his blood, and his blood ran bright for her. His dreams were the flowers of his blood. Hers were more detached and in-human. For centuries a certain type of woman has been rejecting the "animal" in humanity, till now her dreams are abstract, and full of fantasy, and her blood runs in bondage, and her kindness is full of cruelty.[14]

She is made to stand for the whole class of dreaming women; and yet she is a very individual person in her own right. She was, we know, drawn from life, her original being a schoolteacher who was Lawrence's close friend in his Croydon days, and with whom he appears to have had much the same experience as Siegmund has with Helena in the book. So there is some personal feeling behind Lawrence's comments on her character.

But it is not so much sexual coldness on Helena's part that destroys her relationship with Siegmund; it is her complete self-sufficiency, the fact that she doesn't really need him as a person. She needs him only as a dream, and her dream of Siegmund is more than Siegmund himself. He destroys the dream when the painful need of lovers for self-revelation takes hold of him and he tells the story of the courtship of his wife, of their marriage and the death of that marriage. Helena realises that love is not ideal but only temporary; it is her hour of disillusion, dreariness, despair. The Siegmund of her dreams is gone:

Helena had rejected him. She gave herself to her fancies only. For some time she had confused Siegmund with her god. Yesterday she had cried to her ideal lover, and found only Siegmund. It was the spear in the side of his tortured self-respect.[15]

He cannot stay with Helena, he cannot stand life with his wife and children; the only solution he can see is death. Above all, he wants peace: for that he went to Helena, and she brought no peace. He thinks of "the after-death, which to him seemed so wonderfully comforting, full of rest, and reassurance, and renewal . . . He was sure of a wonderful kindness in death, a kindness which really reached right through life, though here he could not avail himself of it."[16] So he leaves Helena, returns home, and commits suicide. Helena's conscience stabs her, but the wound will heal with time.

It is a sombre ending, but most of the story is played out in beautiful surroundings on radiant summer days. Already in *The White Peacock* Lawrence had shown his powers of observation and description of nature, but in this book they are put to much better use, for the Isle of Wight itself is made to play an integral part in the emotions of the lovers:

> In the intense joy and suffering of his realised passion, the island, with its sea and sky, had fused till, like a brilliant bead, all their beauty ran together out of the common ore, and Siegmund saw it naked, saw the beauty of everything naked in the shifting magic of this bead.[17]

Their feelings are affected by the sea, by the sun and its setting, by stars and moonlight and sea-mist at night, by flowers on the downs, and by the tiny life of the rock pools on the shore. Nearly all their talk and togetherness takes place in the open air. "It is all enchanted," Siegmund has to admit even after Helena has cast him off. Indeed, their time together is an escape from everyday reality into an almost mythological world. It is not for nothing that, throughout the book, Wagner and his music are constantly evoked. A sunset evokes the Grail music in *Lohengrin*; even a fog-horn is "something like the call of the horn, across the sea to Tristan"; and Helena, we are told, "for ever hummed fragments of *Tristan*. As she stood on the rocks, she sang, in her little, half-articulate way, bits of Isolde's love, bits of Tristan's anguish, to Siegmund."[18]

The cultural references in Lawrence's early books look curiously archaic today. To give one more example from this novel—Siegmund has hardly settled down in the cottage that the lovers are to share before Helena points out the volume of Nietzsche that she has brought to enliven the stay. We think of Lawrence as being so much a man of our own time that we forget that he was born a Victorian, and that the great influential figures of his youth were Nietzsche, Carlyle, Ruskin, even Herbert Spencer, as prophets; Verlaine and Whitman as poets; the Pre-Raphaelites in art; Wagner and—to be very up-to-date—Debussy as composers. The intellectual life of his student days had not felt the impact of Marx or Freud, any more than the artistic world had felt the impact of Picasso or Stravinsky or Proust. Indeed the great makers of the new art and literature of the twentieth century were mostly men of Lawrence's own generation, too late to influence him or be influenced by him.

Lawrence was not a remarkable technical innovator in the novel: he had no sympathy for the experiments of Proust or Joyce. They seemed to him the dying agony of the novel. "You can hear the death-rattle in their throats. They can hear it themselves. They are listening to it with acute interest, trying to discover whether the intervals are minor thirds or major fourths."[19] Lawrence was perfectly happy to accept the *form* of the novel that Dickens used, but in subject-matter he needed to make a drastic break with the past. It is astonishing how many subjects had been left untouched, or dealt with only superficially, in the brilliant history of English fiction up to 1900. Where, for example, could one find a rendering of working-class family life untouched by sentimentality or condescension or propagandist intent? Where could one find an account of the complete life—mental, spiritual, sexual—of a married couple, or of young men and women growing up?

In his third book, *Sons and Lovers*, Lawrence begins to

extend the boundaries of the novel into this virgin territory. It is the story of his own early life, a story so rich in material that one is grateful that Lawrence did not attempt it as his first book, but waited until he had attained greater mastery of his medium. It represents a very great step forward from *The Trespasser* and *The White Peacock*, which were works of promise rather than of assured achievement. *Sons and Lovers* immediately put Lawrence amongst the leading novelists of his day.

Eastwood, here thinly disguised as Bestwood, set amongst the remains of the old rural England, provides the social and historical background of the book. Neither the countryside nor the men have yet been ruined by mechanical industrialism: the mines are still something of a natural phenomenon and the miner a nocturnal animal ("like a moudiwarp," as Mr Morel says) quite out of place in the daylight world. The story starts with Lawrence's parents, the Mr and Mrs Morel of the book.

They first meet at a dance. She is puritanical, high-minded, educated, from an old "burgher," Congregationalist family that had come down in the world. To the miner Morel, she is a thing of mystery, a lady; and he is an object of equal fascination to her. She is struck by his vividness—his wavy black hair and vigorous black beard, ruddy cheeks and red, moist mouth—and by his rich, ringing laugh and his humour, that is soft, non-intellectual, warm, a kind of gambolling. The description of Morel shows a sensuous apprehension of character that was something quite new in the English novel:

> Therefore the dusky, golden softness of this man's sensuous flame of life, that flowed off his flesh like the flame from a candle, not baffled and gripped into incandescence by thought and spirit as her life was, seemed to her something wonderful, beyond her.[20]

A year later they get married, and for another year Mrs Morel obtains real joy and satisfaction from her marriage.

But the contrast of character that had drawn them together holds the seeds of the ruin of their marriage. "His
nature was purely sensuous, and she strove to make him
moral, religious."[21] He has no sense of responsibility: she
discovers unpaid bills, detects him in lies and evasions.
He begins to neglect her, and (though he had signed the
pledge when he married her) spends more of his spare
time drinking in the pub again.

When the first child arrives, Mrs Morel already is
bitterly disillusioned, and she gives the boy some of the
love that she had once given to her husband. A second
child is born: but all the time her love for her husband is
ebbing away, so that she dreads the arrival of the third
child, and at its birth she feels that she and her husband
are guilty:

> In her arms lay the delicate baby. Its deep blue eyes,
> always looking up at her unblinking, seemed to draw
> her innermost thoughts out of her. She no longer loved
> her husband; she had not wanted this child to come,
> and there it lay in her arms and pulled at her heart.
> She felt as if the navel string that had connected its
> frail little body with hers had not been broken. A wave
> of hot love went over her to the infant. She held it close
> to her face and breast. With all her force, with all her
> soul she would make up to it for having brought it into
> the world unloved. She would love it all the more now
> it was here; carry it in her love. Its clear, knowing eyes
> gave her pain and fear. Did it know all about her?
> When it lay under her heart, had it been listening
> then? Was there a reproach in the look? She felt the
> marrow melt in her bones, with fear and pain.[22]

This third child is Paul Morel.

The children see their father with their mother's eyes,
and all unite against him: only occasionally, when he is
happily engrossed in cobbling boots or mending a kettle,
do the children have any contact with him. His wife's

civilised manners have no effect on him: he prefers to eat his food with a clasp-knife and drink his tea from the saucer; and his grossness and drunkenness only exacerbate his wife's sensitivity. So the children grow up to despise their father, and Mrs Morel determines that her sons will never become miners. They will be educated and (much to their father's disgust) will get "superior" jobs as clerks. The children are brought up as earnest teetotallers and when William, the eldest, starts going to dances his mother violently disapproves. Had she not met Morel at a dance?

Her fears, to some extent, are justified. William's success in business takes him to London, and there at a dance he meets a girl who is a "lady" but spendthrift and scatterbrained. They become engaged, and Mrs Morel sees herself losing the boy on whom she has pinned so many hopes in a marriage that bears all the signs of being more hopelessly a failure than her own. But before he can get married he dies suddenly of pneumonia. It seems the end of everything for her. For months she broods on William; and it is only when Paul himself goes down with pneumonia and has to be nursed that his need restores her to life. From then on her life roots itself in Paul. Her husband having failed her, she needs her sons to be her lovers.

The first part of the book is a brilliant realistic picture of working-class life, of childhood games and illnesses and festivities, of making do on very little money. And although the family is overshadowed by the split between father and mother, there are still times of great happiness. "Home was home and they loved it with a passion of love, whatever the suffering had been."[23]

The theme of the second part of the book is the struggle for Paul's soul between his mother and the girl Miriam, who lives with her family on a small farm a few miles from the Morel home. The real farm (the "Haggs" of the letter quoted on p. 10) and Jessie Chambers, the original of "Miriam", were decisive factors in Lawrence's own development. Years later he wrote: "Whatever I forget, I shall never forget the Haggs . . . it really was a new life began in me there."[24] First it was the life of the farm and the countryside, which he drew upon and described in such loving detail in *The White Peacock*: secondly it was a new spiritual life stimulated by contact with Jessie Chambers, and this paradoxically at odds with the natural life of the countryside. For the very naturalness of country life heightened the girl's spirituality—and here we must return from real life to the novel again:

But, perhaps, because of the continual business of birth and of begetting which goes on upon every farm, Miriam was the more hypersensitive to the matter, and her blood was chastened almost to disgust of the faintest suggestion of such intercourse. Paul took his pitch from her, and their intimacy went on in an utterly blanched and chaste fashion. It could never be mentioned that the mare was in foal.[25]

Mrs Morel, for all her puritanism, was logical, commonsensical, and resolute. But for Miriam and her mother, everything, even a piece of housework, was exalted to the plane of a religious trust. Miriam saw herself as a romantic heroine, the swine-girl who was really a princess, and as she could not be a princess by birth or wealth, "she was mad to have learning whereon to pride herself." So, rather pathetically, she gets Paul to teach her algebra and French and to set exercises for her. In return Miriam and her family "were almost his disciples. They kindled him and made him glow to his work."

There was for him the most intense pleasure in talking about his work to Miriam. All his passion, all his wild blood, went into this intercourse with her, when he talked and conceived his work. She brought forth to him his imaginations. She did not understand, any more than a woman understands when she conceives a child in her womb. But this was life for her and for him.[26]

Miriam urged the artist to life in Paul, but the man she ignored, just as Paul ignored the woman in her. Neither of them could conceive of their relationship as being other than Platonic, a thing of the soul on a high plane of abstraction. After years of intimate friendship, not even a kiss was possible. It was not a case of Paul fighting down sexual desire; he just did not want Miriam like that. "He wished he did. He would have given his head to have felt a joyous desire to marry her and to have her."[27] But "it seemed as if virginity were a positive force which fought and won in both of them."[28] This is the puritan tradition with a vengeance—a fierceness in purity reminiscent of the young Milton. And the reason lies, in this case, with the lovers' mothers. Miriam's had said to her, "There is one thing in marriage that is always dreadful, but you have to bear it." Today this may read like a caricature of Victorian marriage, but at the beginning of the century it obviously represented what was often the painful truth. As Paul reflects:

A good many of the nicest men he knew were like himself, bound in by their own virginity, which they could not break out of. They were so sensitive to their women that they would go without them for ever rather than do them a hurt, an injustice. Being the sons of mothers whose husbands had blundered rather brutally through their feminine sanctities, they were themselves too diffident and shy. They could easier deny themselves than incur any reproach from a woman; for a woman was like their mother, and they were full of the sense of their mother. They preferred themselves to suffer the misery of celibacy, rather than risk the other person.[29]

At last "life itself" overcomes this sensitivity; Paul forces the issue and makes love to Miriam, who sacrifices herself because she loves him. He can only act from brute strength, without thought of her; and this initiation into manhood leaves him with a sense of failure and death. Instead of drawing them together, it puts them apart. Finally Paul decides that Miriam wants not a mate, but a Christ. He tells her that they must break off their relationship, but at the same time he wants to indulge in the luxury of looking back nostalgically on it, on the perfect times they had spent together. But Miriam swears that there were no perfect times, that always he was fighting her off. "He had had a great shock when she had told him that their love had been always a conflict."[30]

But Paul did not have to contend only with the conflict in his love for Miriam; more acute was the fight between Miriam and his mother for his soul. His deepest love was for his mother, and he realised that he was life to her. As long as she lived he could not give himself completely to another woman. Yet his young life, strong and imperious, urged him towards something else. After the break with Miriam, he turns to Clara Dawes. Clara is the type of "new woman" of the period: married, but separated from her husband, she earns her own living and is interested in the Suffragette movement and in educating herself. After Miriam's deep but narrow spirituality, Clara seems trivial and flippant, but she has the warmth and mature womanliness that Miriam lacked. For a time she and Paul are passionately in love; but the consummation of their love brings only momentary satisfaction. For Paul there is the same sort of impersonality about it as there was with Miriam: "It was not Clara. It was something that happened because of her, but it was not her. They were scarcely any nearer each other."[31] Clara, like Miriam, realises that she has no hold over the real and vital Paul. She has served her purpose in the story, and can ignominiously be shuffled off the scene by being reconciled to her weak and worthless husband, after a melodramatic fight between him and Paul.

Meanwhile Paul's mother has died, slowly and painfully; and he is left derelict, in despair. There is no one now to love him or to help him, no mother, no Miriam, no Clara; but the book ends with a rejection of despair and a determination to face the unknown future.

Sons and Lovers has been, and is likely to remain, Lawrence's most popular book. Up to Paul's affair with Clara, the story is almost completely autobiographical. While writing it, Lawrence was in correspondence with Jessie Chambers (the original of Miriam), who helped him by sending her recollections of incidents and emotions from their friendship. Where the novel chiefly deviates from reality is firstly in denying Paul the education that his creator had. Lawrence himself spent only three months as a clerk with a manufacturer of surgical appliances before training to become a teacher, whereas Paul is permanently employed there after leaving school. Secondly, there is no evidence that anything like Paul's affair with Clara actually happened in Lawrence's own life, though several women whom he knew may have supplied ideas for Clara's character.

The book is at its best when it is nearest the truth—in the brilliant early pages on the Morel's family life. In the second part of the book, dominated by the Miriam-Paul relationship, there is more of a sense of strain, because Lawrence is obviously still puzzling out exactly what had gone wrong between them—but the adolescent world is wonderfully evoked. The final Clara episode is the least satisfactory, but the end of the novel is redeemed by the moving account of Mrs Morel's death.

REFERENCES

1. *S.L.*, p. 256.
2. *S.L.*, p. 1.
3. *S.L.C.*, p. 2.
4. *W.P.*, p. 222.
5. *W.P.*, p. 159.
6. *W.P.*, p. 236.
7. *W.P.*, p. 243.
8. *W.P.*, p. 273.
9. *W.P.*, p. 274.
10. *W.P.*, p. 145.
11. *W.P.*, pp. 147, 148.
12. Letter, 30 July, 1908.
13. *T.*, p. 9.
14. *T.*, p. 23.
15. *T.*, p. 101.
16. *T.*, p. 159.
17. *T.*, p. 101.
18. *T.*, p. 166.
19. *S.L.C.*, p. 114.
20. *S.L.*, p. 10.
21. *S.L.*, p. 14.
22. *S.L.*, p. 37.
23. *S.L.*, p. 82.
24. *L.*, p. 761.
25. *S.L.*, p. 162.
26. *S.L.*, p. 202.
27. *S.L.*, p. 278.
28. *S.L.*, p. 278.
29. *S.L.*, p. 279.
30. *S.L.*, p. 299.
31. *S.L.*, p. 354.

CHAPTER II

THE RAINBOW

Lawrence was just twenty-seven when he completed *Sons and Lovers*. Already he had achieved what no English novelist before him had attempted—a complete and comprehensive picture of childhood, adolescence, and young manhood, which had both spiritual depth and vivid circumstantial detail. Of the four archetypal figures which dominated Lawrence's life and work—the sensuous, mindless father; the possessive, loving mother; the yearning, spiritual girl; and the mature woman who brings fulfilment—only the last does not appear in this book: but six months before he finished it she had entered his life.

"Oh," wrote Lawrence only a week or two after he met her, "but she's the woman of a lifetime!" So she was to prove. She was Frieda, wife of Professor Ernest Weekley of Nottingham University, to whom Lawrence had gone for advice about his career. She was six years older than Lawrence and, when they first met, she had already been married for twelve years and had three children. Lawrence said that the university brought him nothing but disillusionment, but in fact it brought him Frieda. It is ironic that the advocate of the passionate consciousness of the common people should have found his mate in the wife of a philologist, leading a life of middle-class comfort in a provincial suburb.

Frieda was in fact a very different person from what her circumstances suggested. She was the daughter of a German aristocrat and soldier, the Baron von Richthofen, and had been brought up in the restricted society of a

conventional upper-class family under the Kaiser. She
had escaped however from army social life by marrying
Weekley, fifteen years older than herself, whose atten-
tions were no doubt flattering to her, and acceptable
to her family, which had a good German respect for
scholars.

There is no evidence that Frieda was very unhappy in
her marriage: she certainly loved her three children. But
she was living only on the surface of life, and Lawrence
gave her "a new world" (as she said), a fulfilment she had
not imagined possible. Equally she brought a new life and
fulfilment to Lawrence. She was a splendidly generous
and vital person, basically simple—not an intellectual,
but a woman of downright commonsense. She was the
anchor of Lawrence's life, and her presence is felt in all
the novels after *Sons and Lovers*: not only is she the wife,
the mate, the beloved, but, almost more importantly, in
both life and fiction, she is the embodiment of superb
sanity, the woman who brings her man back to earth
after his wilder excursions into the unknown, who mocks
his self-importance and puts salt on the tail of his
polemic.

The elopement with Frieda and the completion of
Sons and Lovers, both in the summer of 1912, marked the
end of the first phase of Lawrence's life. For the next two
years the lovers led a wandering existence, chiefly on the
Continent, until Frieda's divorce came through, and they
were able to marry, in July 1914. During this period,
Lawrence was working on the material that was eventually to yield his two greatest books, *The Rainbow* and
Women in Love. Some account of his struggle with his
material—at one time called *The Sisters* and later *The
Wedding Ring*—will be found in a series of letters written
to Edward Garnett in 1913 and 1914. He is sending
Garnett various drafts of the book for criticism, and is
anxious to forewarn him about his intentions, and to
counter his possible objections:

I have no longer the joy in creating vivid scenes, that I
had in *Sons and Lovers*....[1]

All the time, underneath, there is something deep
evolving itself out of me.[2]

You mustn't look in my novel for the old stable *ego* of
the character....[3]

I think it's great—so new, so really a stratum deeper
than I think anybody has ever gone, in a novel.[4]

These statements are still helpful in warning the
reader not to expect a novel in the style of, say, Arnold
Bennett; and such a warning is still required, for anyone
reading *The Rainbow* for the first time must sense the
queerness of the book. It is completely original. Not only
is it unlike any novel that came before it but it is also
quite different in spirit from any of Lawrence's later
books—even its sequel *Women in Love*. It goes very deep,
so deep that previous ideas of "character" in fiction do
not apply because Lawrence is dealing not so much with
individuals as with humanity.

So, while *Sons and Lovers* tells the story of one individual
growing up, *The Rainbow* offers no such clear-cut story
but develops instead its theme of men and women constantly entering new circles of existence and experience
between birth and death. Both books are about growth,
development, but *The Rainbow* is by far the more impersonal and more generalised of the two.

The first paragraphs of the book set out superbly its
world—that of the Brangwen family, who for generations
have lived at the Marsh Farm amongst the water-
meadows of the Derbyshire-Nottinghamshire borders.
They lived with plenty, but without riches, and in tune
with the rhythms of nature:

They felt the rush of the sap in spring, they knew the
wave which cannot halt, but every year throws forward
the seed to begetting, and, falling back, leaves the
young-born on the earth. They knew the intercourse

between heaven and earth, sunshine drawn into the breast and bowels, the rain sucked up in the daytime, nakedness that comes under the wind in autumn, showing the birds' nests no longer worth hiding. Their life and inter-relations were such; feeling the pulse and body of the soil, that opened to their furrow for the grain, and became smooth and supple after their ploughing, and clung to their feet with a weight that pulled like desire, lying hard and unresponsive when the crops were to be shorn away.[5]

And for the men this is enough:

So much warmth and generating and pain and death did they know in their blood, earth and sky and beast and green plants, so much exchange and interchange they had with these, that they lived full and surcharged, their senses full fed, their faces always turned to the heat of the blood, staring into the sun, dazed with looking towards the source of generation, unable to turn round.

But the woman wanted another form of life than this, something that was not blood-intimacy. . . . She faced outwards to where men moved dominant and creative, having turned their back on the pulsing heat of creation, and with this behind them, were set out to discover what was beyond, to enlarge their own scope and range and freedom; whereas the Brangwen men faced inwards to the teeming life of creation, which poured unresolved into their veins.[6]

This is the same situation as that between the miners and their wives in *Sons and Lovers*: the men want no more than their "blood-intimacy," but "the woman was the symbol of that further life which comprised religion and love and morality."[7] So, under the influence of their mothers, the sons idealise all women in their mothers' images. It is so with Tom, the first of the generations of the Brangwens whose life is given to us in any detail. His young manhood is tormented by the disparity between his instinctive desires and his belief that women embody all his most powerful religious impulses. His first sexual experience, with a prostitute at nineteen, leaves him with a "taste of ash and of cold fear . . . lest his relations with woman were going to be no more than this nothingness."[8] He is filled with hatred and fear of sex, combined with constant desire and lustful imaginings. He remains aloof from women but finds excitement in heavy bouts of brandy-drinking; and so his life goes on until his late twenties.

For the first ten thousand words or so, the novel progresses without any very vivid incident and with only one short passage of dialogue, presenting the foreground figure of young Tom, and slowly but richly filling in the background of Midland country life a century ago. But suddenly a strangeness comes over the story: one day on the road Tom passes an unknown woman. They exchange glances: " 'That's her,' he said involuntarily." She is a Polish lady, Lydia Lensky, widow of a refugee doctor, mother of a small girl, and housekeeper for the vicar. Later she comes to Tom's farm to buy butter, and after her first trivial conversation with him:

A daze had come over his mind, he had another centre of consciousness. In his breast, or in his bowels, somewhere in his body, there had started another activity. It was as if a strong light were burning there, and he was blind within it, unable to know anything, except that this transfiguration burned between him and her, connecting them, like a secret power.[9]

They meet occasionally only. Then one night he goes to the vicarage and bluntly proposes. She accepts and they marry. In every way the utter foreignness between them is emphasised. It is not just that their backgrounds are so alien: they have little to talk about, and do not even take very much conscious notice of one another. Yet the hours of remoteness alternate with moments of intense consummation: "He knew her essence. . . . And he seemed to live thus in contact with her, in contact with the unknown, the unaccountable and incalculable."[10]

It is a strange relationship—all the stranger and more "unaccountable" (Lawrence's own word for it) because it is set against the solid tradition of the Brangwens and the concrete details of the farm, of the market, of Tilly the housekeeper; and because it is the experience of an ordinary farmer, whose dullness of wit Lawrence takes care to emphasise. Many readers, I suspect, find this first major episode in the book a puzzling obstacle, as it seems so remote from common experience. But it is obviously a possible human experience. It is the central experience of Tom's life; it is one of the vital experiences of the book, and one with which the other relationships between a man and a woman described are tacitly compared and contrasted.

With so subterranean a relationship, contact may cease as suddenly as it began, and with as little apparent reason. Thus, after some time, Lydia becomes more and more unaware of her husband. "He felt like a broken arch thrust sickeningly out from support. For her response was gone, he thrust at nothing."[11] In these fluctuations of relationship, the reader may find difficulty in precisely comprehending, let alone sharing, the feelings involved. No amount of metaphor can make them memorable or concretely vivid. Lawrence convinces us that he has gone a stratum deeper, but he does not always convincingly present to us what he finds at that level. Where he is triumphantly successful is in the sensuous presentation of the major moments of life—birth, marriage, and death. Thus in the tense hours when his wife is in labour with his first child, and his step-daughter is terrified, blindly crying for her mother and resistant to all attempts at comfort, Tom decides that he will take the child out in the pouring wet night to "give the cows their something-to-eat":

He opened the doors, upper and lower, and they entered into the high, dry barn, that smelled warm even if it were not warm. He hung the lantern on the nail and shut the door. They were in another world now. The light shed softly on the timbered barn, on the whitewashed walls, and the great heap of hay; instruments cast their shadows largely, a ladder rose to the dark arch of a loft. Outside there was the driving rain, inside, the softly-illuminated stillness and calmness of the barn.

Holding the child on one arm, he set about preparing the food for the cows, filling a pan with chopped hay and brewer's grains and a little meal. The child, all wonder, watched what he did. A new being was created in her for the new conditions. Sometimes, a little spasm, eddying from the bygone storm of sobbing, shook her small body. Her eyes were wide and wondering, pathetic. She was silent, quite still.

In a sort of dream, his heart sunk to the bottom, leaving the surface of him still, quite still, he rose with the panful of food, carefully balancing the child on one arm, the pan in the other hand. The silky fringe of the shawl swayed softly, grains and hay trickled to the floor; he went along a dimly-lit passage behind the mangers, where the horns of the cows pricked out of the obscurity. The child shrank, he balanced stiffly, rested the pan on the manger wall, and tipped out the food, half to this cow, half to the next. There was a noise of chains running, as the cows lifted or dropped their heads sharply; then a contented, soothing sound, a long snuffing as the beasts ate in silence.

The journey had to be performed several times. There was the rhythmic sound of the shovel in the barn, then the man returned walking stiffly between

the two weights, the face of the child peering out from
the shawl. Then the next time, as he stooped, she
freed her arm and put it round his neck, clinging soft
and warm, making all easier.

The beasts fed, he dropped the pan and sat down on
a box to arrange the child.

"Will the cows go to sleep now?" she said, catching
her breath as she spoke.

"Yes."

"Will they eat all their stuff up first?"

"Yes. Hark at them."

And the two sat still listening to the snuffing and
breathing of cows feeding in the sheds communicating
with this small barn. The lantern shed a soft, steady
light from one wall. All outside was still in the rain.
He looked down at the silky folds of the paisley shawl.
It reminded him of his mother. She used to go to
church in it. He was back again in the old irrespon-
sibility and security, a boy at home.[12]

This is the sort of passage which, far more than all the
talk about "blood-intimacy," conveys the pulse of life.
We sense and smell the barn, the feeling of space and
light and darkness, the presence of the animals. The
details of the preparation of the food catch the child's
interest, as they do ours, and woo her away from her
blind sorrow; and the contentment of the animals and
the rhythm of Tom's balanced tread brings calm and
makes "all easier." In the house, a new life is starting in
pain and tension: but, outside, life is going on, unchang-
ingly all the time, and Tom is thinking of his own mother
and childhood. And later in the book, in the same barn,
with again the rain slanting down in the darkness outside,
the little girl, Anna, whom Tom had brought in on the
night of childbirth years before, stands now a young
woman in the arms of her lover. " 'I love you, Will, I love
you,' she moaned, 'I love you, Will'."[13] Tom, her step-

father, sees them from the yard, and remembering the
soft, warm weight of the little girl on that night long ago
is black with misery and gloom at the prospect of losing
her. But the cycle of life inevitably goes on.

On the farm, and in the village, the sense of continuity
is strong: the young walk and talk and make love where
their parents and grandparents did. Yet this unchangeable rhythm does not make life any easier for them. Each
generation has to struggle anew up through the circles of
experience, and with each generation the imagery of
"becoming" is renewed. When Tom first met Lydia, he
had "another centre of consciousness"; but after a few
years of marriage they make their "entry into another
circle of existence," pass "through the doorway into the
further space." And when, in the next generation, Anna
meets Will, she feels that "in him the bounds of her experience were transgressed: he was the hole in the wall,
beyond which the sunshine blazed on an outside world."[14]

The courtship of Anna and her cousin Will has none of
the strangeness of that of Tom and Lydia. Their wedding
—Chapter Four of the book—is one of Lawrence's most
splendid scenes: hilarious and serious, bawdy and tender,
at the very heart of English life. In comparison, Dickens
seems too facetious and sentimental, George Eliot too
straitlaced, and Hardy a little too condescending and
nostalgic. Almost better is the description of their honeymoon in their cottage next to the church:

This then was marriage! The old things didn't matter
any more. One got up at four o'clock, and had broth
at teatime and made toffee in the middle of the night.
One didn't put on one's clothes or one did put on one's
clothes. He still was not quite sure it was not criminal.
But it was a discovery to find one might be so supremely
absolved. All that mattered was that he should love
her and she should love him and they should live
kindled to one another, like the Lord in two burning

bushes that were not consumed. And so they lived for the time.[15]

This stands as a picture of absolutely normal marriage against the strange, but deeper, relationship between Tom and Lydia. But it is axiomatic that no Lawrencian marriage should be free from strife—and strife does not mean nagging and petty irritations, but a battle of wills. These battles are always interspersed with quieter times —times of separateness, times of reconciliation, times of joyous reunion. And throughout everything each partner knows that he or she is indissolubly tied to the other.

So with Anna and Will: after the brief honeymoon the struggle begins, and it centres at first on the village church. Will is not a countryman but a designer in a lace-factory, a craftsman with a passion for Gothic architecture; and it is the village church rather than country life that has an irresistible fascination for him. And it is not only the aesthetic delight of the church itself—the stained glass and the carving—but the spirit of mystery and gloom that it embodies. Religion for him has nothing to do with morals and mankind: it is an emotional experience of the infinite, the absolute. He believes in miracles and loves the symbols of religion, while Anna finds the one impossible and the other ridiculous.

The Established Church plays a greater part in this book than in any other. (Lawrence himself was brought up in the Nonconformist tradition, and it is the chapel—severely moral, non-mystical—that stands for religion in his other English novels and stories). The Anglican Church, of course, stands for tradition and continuity, and one of the key passages of the book is that in which Will and Anna visit Lincoln Cathedral. To Will, the Cathedral has the same kind of significance as the natural life of the farm had to his forefathers—and it is described in the same sort of terms:

Between east and west, between dawn and sunset, the

church lay like a seed in silence, dark before germination, silenced after death. Containing birth and death, potential with all the noise and transition of life, the cathedral remained hushed, a great, involved seed, whereof the flower would be radiant life inconceivable, but whose beginning and whose end were the circle of silence. Spanned round with the rainbow, the jewelled gloom folded music upon silence, light upon darkness, fecundity upon death, as a seed folds leaf upon leaf and silence upon the root and the flower, hushing up the secret of all between its parts, the death out of which it fell, the life into which it has dropped, the immortality it involves, and the death it will embrace again.[16]

But Anna resents Will's ecstasies: for her, the altar is barren, and the cathedral a confined place from which one must escape to the freedom of the blue sky outside. And she takes malicious delight in pointing out to Will the sly little faces carved in stone, winking and leering, suggesting "the many things that had been left out of the great concept of the church."[17] (In this conflict there is something parallel to Lawrence's own situation—he the "passionately religious man," anxious for a faith, with Frieda constantly mocking his more spiritual flights and bringing him firmly down to earth. This situation is more fully exploited in a later novel, *Kangaroo*).

The disillusionment that Anna's mockery brings on has a decisive effect on Will. The cathedral had been an absolute in a world of chaos but now he had lost his absolute, and the loss makes him a more superficial person. He remains "uncreated," slightly ashamed, having failed to find real expression. For Anna, "if her soul had found no utterance, her womb had": she becomes absorbed in her children. But neither Anna nor Will develops much more. "Becoming" is a major theme of the book, and not to "become" represents failure (another major theme)— Anna's failure, Will's failure, Lydia Lensky's first hus-

band's failure. Lydia herself and Tom, the older generation, attained at least fulfilment with one another,
though Tom feels he has achieved nothing beyond that:

> Was his life nothing? Had he nothing to show, no
> work? He did not count his work, anybody could have
> done it. What had he known, but the long, marital
> embrace with his wife! Curious, that this was what his
> life amounted to! At any rate, it was something, it was
> eternal. He would say so to anybody, and be proud of
> it. He lay with his wife in his arms, and she was still his
> fulfilment, just the same as ever. And that was the be-
> all and the end-all. Yes, and he was proud of it.[18]

Anna and Will do not achieve this "long, marital embrace." After the rapture of their honeymoon there are
some years of increasing coldness and strife between them,
until they flare up into a period of pure lust—lust, which
is to Lawrence a negative, deathly thing ("they had no
conscious intimacy, no tenderness of love"). And when
this has died down, Will finds what fulfilment he can in
his craft and Anna in bringing up her nine children. But
they do not have the real marital fulfilment of the older
generation.

Ursula, the eldest of their children, carries the story on
into the third generation. She and Will are passionately
devoted to one another, and this intense father-daughter
attachment is a pair with the mother-son relationship in
Sons and Lovers. Indeed, the last half of *The Rainbow* does
for a girl what the earlier novel did for a boy—traces her
life from childhood through adolescence, faith and loss
of faith, first love and loss of love, up to adulthood. At the
end Ursula is left, like Paul Morel, still in the process of
"becoming", with much experience behind her, but still
"uncreated" in face of the unknown future.

It seems probable that the second part of the book,
dealing with Ursula, was written first, very soon after the
completion of *Sons and Lovers*. The theme is very similar

and is presented with the same particularity of the details of childhood, in contrast to the greater impersonality and vagueness of the first part of *The Rainbow*. Moreover, Ursula is of Lawrence's own generation, and to a certain extent she shares Lawrence's experiences. Her grandfather's youth was confined to life on the farm, her father's was devoted to craftsmanship and his passion for the Church, but her own is dominated by education—first as a pupil, then as a student, then as a teacher. It is a progression that may, at first sight, appear to be towards enlightenment, and Ursula is certainly a more complex person than her grandfather; but it is also, Lawrence suggests, a progression away from a natural, profound life to a more mechanical, superficial one.

The young Ursula has the same passion for religion as her adored father. She, too, craves the ecstasy; but, where Will's was an impersonal male passion for the absolute, hers is a girl's intensely personal emotion centred on the love of Jesus, and inextricably mixing sensuality and spirituality:

Early in the year, when the lambs came, and shelters were built of straw, and on her uncle's farm the men sat at night with a lantern and a dog, then again there swept over her this passionate confusion between the vision world and the weekday world. Again she felt Jesus in the countryside. Ah, he would lift up the lambs in his arms! Ah, and she was the lamb. . . . Jesus—the vision world—the everyday world—all mixed inextricably in a confusion of pain and bliss. It was almost agony, the confusion, the inextricability. Jesus, the vision, speaking to her, who was non-visionary! And she would take his words of the spirit and make them to pander to her own carnality.[19]

This is Ursula at sixteen. But now she falls in love with Anton Skrebensky. He, like Ursula's grandmother, is of Polish descent, though now a subaltern in the British army. He brings a sense of the great outside world to the enclosed life of the Brangwens, and at first his love affair with Ursula is idyllic and rapturous. But he has no individual soul; his life is purely on the surface, circumscribed by his duties and the established order of things. Ursula in exasperation tells him:

> "It seems to me . . . as if you weren't anybody—as if there weren't anybody there, where you are. Are you anybody, really? You seem like nothing to me."[20]

But she still loves him romantically, and when he goes off to the South African war, she is left desolate.

Then gradually her romantic dreams turn towards one of her schoolmistresses, Winifred Inger, and the two fall passionately in love. Her teacher represents an ideal, another form of existence. She is "the modern young woman," independent, self-possessed, clever, and graceful. The two delight in one another, swimming, rowing, endlessly discussing politics and philosophy. But Ursula at last is nauseated by their physical intimacy, at sharing the unnatural life of the elder woman, and begins to plan marriage for her. Instinctively she thinks of an uncle, Tom, who manages a colliery, and she takes Miss Inger to stay with him. The incredible ugliness and desolation of the colliery district is vividly conveyed. Even the large library of Uncle Tom's house, which might seem a haven of enlightenment, gives a sense of "hard, mechanical activity. . . 'looking out on the hideous abstraction of the town, and at the green meadows and rough country beyond and at the great, mathematical colliery on the other side."[21]

Uncle Tom sees in Miss Inger "a kinship with his own dark corruption." "His real mistress was the machine, and the real mistress of Winifred was the machine."[22] So they marry, and Ursula, who had loved them both, turns against them, hating their machine-dominated lives.

She has fought Skrebensky's "duty"; now she decides

that she must fight the great machine. She returns home, to another fight—against her mother. Anna Brangwen is now about to have her ninth child and knows only what to Ursula seems "the close physical limited life of herded domesticity." Ursula's young ardours and aspirations are ridiculed by her mother. Skrebensky's love is only a memory, and a dead memory, for she feels her power of love is dead after Winifred. She is seventeen. All that she can do to escape from home is to teach. So, like Lawrence himself, she takes a teaching job in Ilkeston.

While most of *The Rainbow* deals with the spiritual, rather than the social, history of England, the story of Ursula's teaching days is a detailed picture (based on Lawrence's own experience) of what an elementary school was like at the beginning of this century. We see it, smell it, and hear it. And it is another bitter disillusionment for Ursula. There are, in one huge room, three classes each of fifty or sixty children and one of these Ursula has to teach. How is any vital contact possible with a class of fifty-five children? The only education possible is summed up in two sentences: "Miss Harby was a splendid teacher. She could keep order and inflict knowledge on a class with remarkable efficiency."[23] The irony of this is Dickensian, and indeed the schoolroom is in the same utilitarian tradition as the schoolroom in *Hard Times*, where the little pitchers waited to have knowledge poured into them. If anything, it is a crueller place. Not only does it have the task "of compelling many children into one disciplined, mechanical set, reducing the whole set to an automatic state of obedience and attention and then of commanding their acceptance of various pieces of knowledge,"[24] but this compulsion is backed up by brute force. Ursula believes that she can make the whole thing personal, that she can offer her class a human relationship, and never use compulsion. But she fails; it is a fight between her and the class, and she can survive only by resorting to brute force herself.

After two years of teaching she goes to Nottingham University. With all her usual idealism, she looks forward to it as a temple of knowledge where the professors are priests; but by her second year the university had become a "warehouse of dead unreality," concerned only with material success. Ursula's young life is a pilgrim's progress of disillusionment: as each promising new vista opens she soon finds her deepest human feelings affronted by the deadly mechanical, the conventional, or the purely physical.

> Always the shining doorway ahead; and then, upon approach, always the shining doorway was a gate into another ugly yard, dirty and active and dead. Always the crest of the hill gleaming ahead under heaven: and then, from the top of the hill only another sordid valley full of amorphous, squalid activity.
>
> No matter! Every hill-top was a little different, every valley was somehow new.[25]

To this situation Skrebensky returns after six years' absence: she feels it will be a new beginning. She finds him physically very attractive: they become lovers and arrange to marry. But she can love him only physically, superficially: in the real depths there is no contact. He is going to India as one of the ruling class, and Ursula is shut dead against such a life. They part.

So she is left quite alone, and this by her own choice. She has even lost her roots in the country, for Will, her father, has become a handiwork-teacher, and the family have moved to an ugly colliery village. Skrebensky has left her pregnant, and after a miscarriage she suffers a temporary breakdown. But in this winter of her soul, she can sense the future life evolving:

> She was the naked, clear kernel thrusting forth the clear, powerful shoot, and the world was a bygone winter, discarded, her mother and father and Anton,

and college and all her friends, all cast off like a year
that has gone by, whilst the kernel was free and naked
and striving to take new root.[26]

The novel ends, on a note of optimism, with Ursula's
vision of the rainbow, symbolising the earth's new architecture, a change of heart. It is as inconclusive as the
ending of *Sons and Lovers*, and for the same reason. Not
only the main character in the book, but Lawrence himself, had passed through one phase of life and was faced
with an unknown future. It needed another, quite
different book to chart the next phase.

Lawrence was still in his twenties when he finished *The
Rainbow*, and the achievement is astonishing. Not only is
life presented a stratum deeper than before; it is also
presented in great variety. Lawrence does not show us
just one sort of sensuality or mechanical activity, but a
number. He probes deeply not just one relationship between a man and a woman, but several; and he does the
same with the relations of parent and child, and the
relations of men and women to God and to nature. And
in every case the quality of the experiences is being
evaluated and placed, never obtrusively by the novelist
himself, but implicitly, in the course of the action, and in
their effect on the lives and characters of the people involved. We do not know the characters of *The Rainbow* in
the way in which we know the characters of, say, *Pickwick
Papers*, but at the end of the book we know ourselves
better, we know life better—and not just English life of
the nineteenth century, but life anywhere today.

The faults of the book are those found to a greater or
lesser degree in all Lawrence's novels, faults due to going
on too long and too insistently. He hammers away too
much at many of the episodes and experiences presented
(Will's devotion to religion, the teaching section, the
Ursula-Skrebensky stalemate), when he has in fact
already summed them up dramatically in vivid scenes

(the visit to Lincoln cathedral, Ursula thrashing a boy, the episode with the bargemen and Skrebensky) that the more abstract commentary becomes superfluous. Lawrence did not always surmount the difficulty inherent in exploring the depths of human personality and relations —the danger of falling into abstractions. One possible way out of the difficulty lies in myth-making (as obviously illustrated by the Freudian take-over of Greek mythology); another is to find a symbol of "objective correlative" of an inner state. It was this latter way that Lawrence in fact took in his next book, with remarkable success.

REFERENCES

1. *L.*, p. 177.
2. *L.*, p. 190.
3. *L.*, p. 198.
4. *L.*, p. 111.
5. *R.*, p. 2.
6. *R.*, p. 3.
7. *R.*, p. 13.
8. *R.*, p. 14.
9. *R.*, p. 33.
10. *R.*, p. 55.
11. *R.*, p. 60.
12. *R.*, pp. 74–5.
13. *R.*, p. 114.

14. *R.*, p. 109.
15. *R.*, pp. 146–7.
16. *R.*, pp. 198–9.
17. *R.*, p. 201.
18. *R.*, p. 124.
19. *R.*, p. 285.
20. *R.*, p. 309.
21. *R.*, p. 345.
22. *R.*, p. 349.
23. *R.*, p. 385.
24. *R.*, p. 382.
25. *R.*, p. 436.
26. *R.*, p. 492.

CHAPTER III

WOMEN IN LOVE

Women in Love grew out of the same material as *The Rainbow*, material written round the character of Ursula, but the two books contrast at nearly every point. Ursula and her younger sister Gudrun (who hardly appeared in *The Rainbow*) are the two main woman characters of the later book. They are now both in their mid-twenties, both teachers in the local grammar school, living with their family in the small mining town of Beldover. The change of scene symbolises the change of mood in this book— away from the traditional village sanctities and the eternal rhythms of natural life. In Beldover Lawrence for the first time exposes the full hideousness of the industrial landscape. This had appeared only very briefly in *The Rainbow* (in the Uncle Tom-Winifred Inger passage), and hardly at all in *The White Peacock* or *Sons and Lovers*, although all these books are set in the same part of England. It seems that when Lawrence actually lived there, or had only recently left, the ugliness had not struck him; but, as he saw more of the world, he, like Gudrun in this book, "shrank cruelly from this amorphous ugliness."[1] Indeed, the further Lawrence moved in time and space from the surroundings of his youth, the stronger his condemnation of them became; and it finally reached its climax in *Lady Chatterley's Lover*, written when Lawrence had not lived in that part of England for many years. His horror does not stop at the external physical aspects of the place, but extends to the people who live there. They too, and their lives, are ugly and meaningless. Lawrence for the first time conveys his feeling of dislike, amounting almost to illness, for the mass of mankind. And the common people, who were the life-blood of *Sons and Lovers*, are now seen only in the mass, leading barren lives in barren surroundings. He has forgotten, or does not choose to remember, that in these seemingly drab homes he and his family and friends led the very intense life of his youth. So, in this book, Ursula's own parents, Will and Anna, whose courtship and marriage and honeymoon were given to us so vividly in *The Rainbow*, are now dismissed by their daughters:

"When I think of their lives—father's and mother's, their love and their marriage, and all of us children, and our bringing up—would you have such a life, Prune?"

"I wouldn't, Ursula".

"It all seems so *nothing*—their two lives—there's no meaning in it".[2]

This is partly every child's cry against his parents, but it is also symptomatic of the spirit of the book. Home is rejected, a settled family life is rejected, possessions are rejected. While *The Rainbow* is a novel of roots and slow organic growth and life, *Women in Love* is a book of upheaval, escape, of coming to the end of things, of death. It is psychically a stage beyond: it is no longer a question of "becoming," it is a question of "Look! we have come through—but what do we do now?"

The changed spirit is reflected, too, in the construction of the book. *The Rainbow* is a narrative, flowing along like life and with some of the same vagueness and even tedium: *Women in Love* is much more definite, a drama proceeding by a series of short, precise episodes, self-contained but interrelated. This book answers the criticism that Lawrence had no sense of form, for only a great architectonic intelligence could comprehend so much of life and present it in one novel with such economy, vividness and brilliance of motivation.

At the beginning of the book, Ursula and Gudrun are discussing marriage; they feel that it would be an intolerable state for them. Then, ironically enough, they set off to see the wedding of a daughter of the Crich family, who own the mines of the district and are the local aristocracy of wealth, if not of breeding. There they watch Gerald, the son of the house, handsome, fair, sunburnt, "almost too well-dressed." Gudrun, who has never seen him before, lights on him at once. "A strange transport took possession of her . . . she was tortured with desire to see him again."[3] There, too, is Gerald's best friend Rupert Birkin, rather self-conscious and out-of-place at a conventional wedding. Ursula already knows him slightly as a school inspector, and feels that there is some kinship between them. "He piqued her, attracted her, and annoyed her."[4] Between Gerald and Rupert there is "a strange perilous intimacy which was either hate or love, or both."[5] Amongst the other wedding guests is Hermione, daughter of a baronet, "a woman of the new school, full of intellectuality and heavy, nerve-worn with consciousness."[6] She and Birkin had been lovers for years, but "he fought her off, he always fought her off."[7] It is the old Paul-Miriam relationship on a more sophisticated level.

These people are all presented in the first chapter, and the rest of the book is a working-out of their relationships. This is done against a wide variety of backgrounds, each of which has its influence on the characters concerned. Thus the first scene takes place in Ursula's schoolroom. Birkin (closely pursued by Hermione) comes to watch a nature-study lesson, and this gives rise to a discussion on education, on knowledge versus the unconscious, in which the three participants become emotionally involved with one another. The next important episode sees Gerald Crich and Rupert Birkin immersed in Bohemian life in London, where the themes are sex and art. Immediately the scene shifts again from the unsettled, promiscuous life of second-rate artists to the graciousness of Hermione's Georgian country house, set in its park amongst the green hills of Derbyshire "as final as an old aquatint."

Hermione has invited Ursula and Gudrun for the week-end, together with Gerald and Birkin and a number of other guests who are depicted with wonderful irony— Hermione's brother—the bachelor M.P., "striding romantically like a Meredith hero who remembers Disraeli,"[8] or Sir Joshua, "a learned, dry Baronet of fifty, who was always making witticisms and laughing at them heartily in a harsh horse-laugh,"[9] and who is seen by Gudrun "as a flat bottle, containing tabloids of compressed liberty."[10] The whole atmosphere of the talk— serious, powerful, anarchistic—is vividly conveyed. Ursula and Gudrun find elation and satisfaction in it all, but at the same time realise its "consuming, destructive mentality," its lack of connexion with vital life. The chapter is a brilliant piece of social description, but it is also far more than that. Lawrence is not just saying (as Aldous Huxley might): "Look, I know what it is like to spend a week-end in a political-artistic country house. I will describe it amusingly for you and reproduce the brilliant talk." He is gradually bringing together the two sisters with Birkin and Gerald, he is unravelling the relationship between the two men and their search for a solution to the problem of living—Gerald half wanting a mistress, half wedded to his work, Birkin seeing marriage as a panacea. The chapter ends in drastic action as Hermione, driven beyond endurance by Birkin, makes a murderous attack on him with a paperweight. From this melodramatic scene, he escapes, shaken, to the countryside. "Here was his world, he wanted nobody and nothing but the lovely, subtle, responsive vegetation, and himself, his own living self."[11]

A later chapter, with the same self-contained air, illuminating quite another aspect of English life and yet having a vital bearing on the story is entitled "The Industrial Magnate." This is the story of the relationship between the Crich family as mine-owners and the miners. It begins with Gerald's father, a man with all the Victorian virtues, constant to charity, loving his workers even better than himself, believing that they will inherit the earth, and that he must gravitate towards their lives if he is to move nearer to God. There comes a crisis in the industry when the employers lock out the miners for refusing to accept lower wages. Gerald's father, in loyalty to the employers' federation, is compelled to close his pits and deny the means of life to his own men. He had wanted to be a pure Christian, one and equal with all men, yet he is also a great industrialist and knows perfectly well that he must preserve his interests and keep his authority. He had wanted the industry to be run on love, and so this state of war breaks his heart.

When Gerald grows up and enters the business he radically alters the situation. He cares nothing for equality or Christian attitudes of love and self-sacrifice; he knows that efficiency is everything in industry and if efficiency is to be achieved, sentiment and emotion must be forgotten. Experts are brought in, the latest methods and machinery are introduced, expenditure is cut, and old charities, such as free coal for widows, are abolished. But the men submit:

Gerald was their high priest, he represented the religion they really felt. His father was forgotten already. There was a new world, a new order, strict, terrible, inhuman, but satisfying in its very destructiveness. The men were satisfied to belong to the great and wonderful machine, even whilst it destroyed them. It was what they wanted. It was the highest that man had produced, the most wonderful and superhuman. . . . It was the first great step in undoing, the first great phase of chaos, the substitution of the mechanical principle for the organic, the destruction of the organic purpose, the organic unity, and the subordination of every organic unit to the great mechanical purpose.[12]

Gerald succeeds in making the whole system so perfect that he is hardly necessary any more. So he has come to the end of everything—the perfection of mechanical activity—and behind the healthy mask of his face is only fear and sterility. He knows that his only way to salvation is through some relationship—and not a purely sexual one—with a woman, and he is drawn to Gudrun. His father is dying and thinks only of the happiness of his youngest daughter, who is still a child; he decides that the best way of ensuring that happiness is for Gudrun to come to the house and help her with her drawing and modelling. The situation is ironic: at a time when Gudrun had been planning to leave the district and go abroad, she and Gerald are brought close together, not by their own volition, but by a father's love for his daughter: and it is the father's death that makes them lovers, for it reduces Gerald to the depths of despair, from which he can find release only in Gudrun's arms:

He had come for vindication. She let him hold her in his arms, clasp her close against him. He found in her an infinite relief. Into her he poured all his pent-up darkness and corrosive death, and he was whole again. It was wonderful, marvellous, it was a miracle. This was the ever-recurrent miracle of his life, at the knowledge of which he was lost in an ecstasy of relief and wonder. And she, subject, received him as a vessel filled with his bitter potion of death. She had no power at this crisis to resist. The terrible frictional violence of death filled her, and she received it in an ecstasy of subjection, in throes of acute, violent sensation.[13]

In love as in business, Gerald is selfish, efficient, unemotional and ruthless. He is a successful lover in the same way as he is a successful mine-owner; and in both activities he is a failure, unable to find happiness. Lawrence, with wonderful art, suggests not only the subtle complications and ironic coincidences that change the course of human affairs, but also the inextricable relations between the public and the private life, between the great colliery that dominates the district and Gerald and Gudrun in bed together.

In contrast to Gerald, his friend Rupert Birkin has practically no public life. We know he is a school inspector, but we are never told his feelings about his work and it seems to have no effect on his private life. For the purposes of the book Birkin must not be an independent gentleman, nor an artist—he must earn a living yet have the maximum of freedom. It is his freedom rather than his work that is important. He is essentially a rootless, classless person, without family, his character wavering, lambent yet instinct with life. It would be wrong to see him as a self-portrait of Lawrence, but he certainly possesses many of the same traits, both lovable and less lovable:

> There was his wonderful, desirable life-rapidity, the rare quality of an utterly desirable man: and there was at the same time this ridiculous, mean effacement into a Salvator Mundi and a Sunday-school teacher, a prig of the stiffest type.[14]

This is Ursula on Birkin and it might well be—probably was—Frieda on Lawrence. (One must give Lawrence due credit for self-knowledge and self-criticism, but even more credit must be due to Frieda, for making him aware of his absurdities and excesses.) Birkin's demands on Ursula certainly at times seem absurd and excessive, as in the following exchange between them:

> "What I want is a strange conjunction with you—" he said quietly; "—not meeting and mingling;—you are

quite right:—but an equilibrium, a pure balance of two single beings:—as the stars balance each other."

She looked at him. He was very earnest, and earnestness was always rather ridiculous, commonplace, to her. It made her feel unfree and uncomfortable. Yet she liked him so much. But why drag in the stars?[15]

And later Gerald and Gudrun join in the criticism:

"He says," she added, with a grimace of irony, "that you can find an eternal equilibrium in marriage, if you accept the unison, and still leave yourself separate, don't try to fuse."

"Doesn't inspire me," said Gerald.

"That's just it," said Gudrun.

"I believe in love, in a real *abandon*, if you're capable of it," said Gerald.

"So do I," said she.

"And so does Rupert, too—though he is always shouting."

"No," said Gudrun. "He won't abandon himself to the other person. You can't be sure of him. That's the trouble I think."

"Yet he wants marriage! Marriage—*et puis?*"

"Le paradis!" mocked Gudrun.[16]

Birkin himself has moments of doubt:

Why bother! Why strive for a coherent, satisfied life? Why not drift on in a series of accidents—like a picaresque novel? Why not? Why bother about human relationships? Why take them seriously—male or female? ... And yet, still, he was damned and doomed to the old effort at serious living.[17]

This is surely Lawrence speaking as well as Birkin, and defining an attitude to literature as well as to life, pointing the difference between the quality of living represented in Lawrence's work and that represented in the picaresque novel.

Birkin is not sure himself exactly what he is seeking but it is something beyond love, something mystical. He is perfectly clear about what he *does not* want: "'I don't want your good looks'," he tells Ursula, "'and I don't want your womanly feelings'."[18] Neither does he want the "hot narrow intimacy between man and wife";[19] at all costs he must avoid the possessiveness of women and their desire for domination. "The thought of love, marriage and children, and a life together, in the horrible privacy of domestic and connubial satisfaction, was repulsive"[20] —in fact, the thought of the family life so vividly depicted in *Sons and Lovers* and *The Rainbow*.

But the problem does not end with women. "He saw himself confronted with another problem—the problem of love and eternal conjunction between two men. Of course this was necessary—it had been a necessity inside himself all his life—to love a man purely and fully."[21] Throughout the book Birkin tries to achieve some such conjunction with Gerald, an attempt which reaches its climax in the scene where the two men wrestle naked on the floor. We recollect the scene in *The White Peacock* where George and Cyril swim together. Yet it seems certain that Lawrence had no homosexual leanings: indeed the whole point of this important relationship with another man was that it should be *non-sexual*, a brotherhood. "We are mentally, spiritually, intimate, therefore we should be more or less physically intimate too—it is more whole."[22] But where Birkin thinks of love between men, Gerald thinks only of friendship, and the "eternal conjunction" is never achieved between them.

Birkin's trouble (and perhaps Lawrence's, too) is wanting all relationships with other people—men or women— entirely on his own terms. Ursula falls deeply in love with him, but (as we have seen) is far from being blind to his faults and far from submitting to his will. She mocks his ideas of an impersonal relationship beyond the emotional, loving plane—ideas which are no basis for marriage; and, more positively, warms and comforts his soul "at the beautiful light of her nature." She wants to give him everything, but, as she complains, "how can I, you don't love me. You only want your own ends. You don't want to serve *me*, and yet you want me to serve you. It is so one-sided."²³ But this episode again ends with them in each other's arms: "it was such peace and heavenly freedom, just to hold her and kiss her gently, and not to have any thoughts or any desires or any will. . . ."²⁴

Birkin at last gives up as impossible the idea of mystic relationship, and settles for "the way of freedom"—

. . . the individual soul taking precedence over love and desire for union, stronger than any pangs of emotion, a lovely state of free proud singleness, which accepted the obligation of the permanent connection with others, and with the other, submits to the yoke and leash of love, but never forfeits its own proud individual singleness, even while it loves and yields.²⁵

It is a way out that Birkin arrives at after much solitary speculation. On achieving it, he immediately sets off to propose to Ursula. It is, indeed, a rather mental way, a somewhat selfish and priggish way of being spurred to marriage. And Ursula refuses to be rushed. She wants to abandon herself finally, "unspeakably," to him, but only on condition that he loves her with the same self-abandon; and she knows that he would never abandon himself finally to her. "She believed that love far surpassed the individual. He said that the individual was *more* than love, or than any relationship."²⁶

There is a final scene of anger between them, after the proposal, when Birkin is driving Ursula in his car. Birkin says that he must get back to see Hermione for the last time, although everything is over between them. Ursula accuses him of still wanting his old deathly relationship with her; he wants his "spiritual brides" and wants to

marry Ursula only for "daily use." And Birkin admits
that in a way it is true; but

> was not Ursula's way of emotional intimacy, emotional
> and physical; was it not just as dangerous as Hermione's
> abstract spiritual intimacy? . . . Hermione saw herself
> as the perfect Idea, to which all men must come: and
> Ursula was the perfect Womb, the bath of birth, to
> which all men must come! And both were horrible.[27]

They have stopped the car to argue, and Ursula walks
away, but after a time drifts desultorily, wistfully back,
bringing him a flower. Birkin's feelings get the better of
his ideas: "a hot passion of tenderness for her filled his
heart."[28] They come together in perfect happiness. They
will marry. When they stop for tea in the hotel at Southwell, she kneels before him:

> She closed her hands over the full, rounded body of his
> loins, as he stooped over her, she seemed to touch the
> quick of the mystery of darkness that was bodily him.
> She seemed to faint beneath, and he seemed to faint,
> stooping over her. It was a perfect passing away for
> both of them, and at the same time the most intolerable
> accession into being, the marvellous fullness of im-
> mediate gratification, overwhelming, outflooding from
> the source of the deepest life-force, the darkest, deepest,
> strangest life-source of the human body, at the back
> and base of the loins.[29]

Yet some of the force of this final coming together is
marred by repetition, marred by the fact that Gudrun
had felt an almost identical emotion for Gerald, when he
was practically a stranger to her:

> Oh, and the beauty of the subjection of his loins, white
> and dimly luminous as he climbed over the side of
> the boat, made her want to die, to die. The beauty of
> his dim and luminous loins as he climbed into the boat,

his back rounded and soft—ah, this was too much for her, too final a vision. She knew it, and it was fatal. The terrible hopelessness of fate, and of beauty, such beauty![30]

Lawrence surely intended that much greater significance should attach to the final coming-together of Ursula and Birkin (leading to marriage) than to the preliminary episode in the Gudrun's affair with Gerald, but the element of jargon common to both renders them almost indistinguishable in quality.

One might say that the only difference between these two passages is that one is about a man in a pair of white flannels who had been in the water, while the other is about a man wearing darker trousers and standing in a hotel room awaiting tea.

Tea occurs at several of the vital points of *Women in Love*. In the midst of a previous verbal battle to the death between Ursula and Birkin tea appeared:

"What *good* things to eat!" she cried.
"Take your own sugar," he said.
He handed her her cup. He had everything so nice, such pretty cups and plates, painted with mauve lustre and green, also shapely bowls and glass plates, and old spoons, on a woven cloth of pale grey and black and purple.[31]

And, likewise, immediately after the further description of Ursula and Birkin in the hotel room at Southwell ("from the smitten rock of the man's body . . . further in mystery than the phallic source, came the floods of ineffable darkness and ineffable riches"), tea arrives and Ursula again exclaims: "What *good* things! How noble it looks!—Shall I pour out the tea?"[32] And we are told how "the tea-pot poured beautifully from a proud slender spout."

These passages are not picked out to poke fun at Lawrence; and, in fact, the effect of bathos is hardly noticed in reading them. But they illustrate a method of procedure that Lawrence consciously or unconsciously adopted in the book—the alternation of passages of "thought," of intellectual discussion and psychic feeling with minute description of everyday things—crockery, cutlery, and, above all, dress. Every reader of the book remembers the descriptive detail lavished particularly on the various outfits worn by Ursula, Gudrun, and Hermione. It is as if Lawrence is anxious to anchor down his more high-flown balloons with solid detail of normal everyday objects. In fact these descriptions serve also as a criticism of the higher flights, just as Ursula's mockery puts Birkin's rodomontades in their place. The method is very successful; we remember the details of the lovers having tea at Southwell, when we have forgotten whose loins it was that were being caressed, and what "electric passion" the caresser felt.

A similar and obviously conscious device is the use of symbolism. Thus Gerald's "will" is exemplified in the scene where he struggles with his terrified horse at a level crossing. Animals are again used to illustrate human situations in the chapters called "Rabbit," and "Mino" (a cat). Another whole symbolic chapter is called "A Chair," where Ursula and Birkin, about to be married, go to the jumble market in the colliery town, and decide to buy a chair, which is described in lyrical detail. Not only is it a beautiful chair in its own right, but is a relic of a better time. Birkin holds forth:

"When I see that clear, beautiful chair, and I think of England, even Jane Austen's England—it had living thoughts to unfold even then, and pure happiness in unfolding them. And now, we can only fish among the rubbish heaps for the remnants of their old expression. There is no production in us now, only sordid and foul mechanicalness."[33]

But Ursula hates the past, and Birkin hates possessions; and, having bought the chair, they decide to give it to a young working-class couple who are standing by—they, too, are about to be married, and the girl is already pregnant. They and the chair represent all that Birkin does not want—the family, the home, possessions.

In such ways as these the long abstract passages that characterised *The Rainbow* are avoided. Nearly everything is made more dramatic and concrete in this book. But there remain some passages that seem nonsensical. Thus, at one point, Birkin is described as being "in pure opposition to everything."[34] "Opposition" one knows; "pure opposition" one can imagine; but "pure opposition to *everything*" is surely an incomprehensible state.

With Birkin and Ursula at last married, if not settled, interest inevitably turns more on Gerald and Gudrun. Gudrun is a little jealous of Ursula, who has found an extraordinary man to be her husband. She wants marriage but finds all men impossible. Even in Gerald's strong and violent love, she is not satisfied: "To marry one must have a free-lance or nothing, a comrade in arms, a Glücksritter. A man with a position in the social world—well, it's just impossible, impossible."[35] Birkin supplies the gloss: "Gudrun! She's a born mistress, just as Gerald is a born lover."[36]

Then the whole scene is wonderfully transposed to the Continent. Gerald suggests that the four of them should go to Austria; Gudrun, after some demur, agrees. They delight in the escape to the unknown, escape from England, "where the damper is never lifted off one." There, high amongst the mountains with their winter snow and ice, Gudrun feels that she has reached her place, her shrine—and Gerald has already lost her. Watching him with the women at the hotel, she realises that he is naturally promiscuous, and prepares to fight him; one of them must triumph over the other. She still has moments of wonder at him, can dream of him as the man to solve the problem of industrialism in the modern world, with "his force of will and power of comprehending the actual world."[37] But she mocks at herself for her dreams. She is really completely cynical. Yet she is, above all, an artist, and in the snow-bound Austrian hotel she meets the final, and perhaps most wonderful, creation of this astonishing book—the sculptor Loerke. He is a man from the lowest depths of life, brought up in poverty and degradation. He is the rock bottom of life, the man without illusions, the man without social position. Gudrun is fascinated and a bond grows between them as they discuss their art together: the others—Ursula, Gerald, Birkin—tend to be repelled. But through art Gudrun and Loerke find that impersonal relationship which Birkin needed: "*I* and my art, they have *nothing* to do with each other. My art stands in another world, I am in this world,"[38] says Gudrun.

All the time she is fighting off Gerald: she tells him that she never really felt love for him, only pity, and gets him to admit that he has never loved her. "Try to love me a little more and to want me a little less,"[39] she says, but her tone is half-contemptuous as well as half-coaxing. But "his passion was awful to her, tense and ghastly, and impersonal, like a destruction, ultimate."[40] Throughout the novel, images of death have been connected with Gerald; and at last, in an encounter with Gudrun and Loerke in the snow, he sees his chance to kill her. "Oh what bliss, at last, what satisfaction, at last!"[41] But the moment passes—"I don't want it, really,"[42] was the last confession of disgust in his soul. Consumed by the death-wish, he yet struggles on and up through the snow, till he falls and is killed.

But Ursula and Birkin had already left before the barren tragedy. Ursula had wanted to leave the snow, to go south. As Birkin had foretold, they are to be wanderers on the face of the earth. It is as if both of them now tied to each other feel the need for a greater liberty in travel; before marriage, one place was liberty enough.

There had been an enormous advance in spiritual and artistic power in the few years between *Sons and Lovers* and *Women in Love*. If the former is Lawrence's *Romeo and Juliet*, the latter is his *Antony and Cleopatra*. One re-reads *Sons and Lovers* with a sense of remembered pleasure: how good it still is. One re-reads *Women in Love* with a sense of new discovery: how much more there is in it than one found before.

The differences between the books are not only differences of artistic maturity; they also reflect the remarkable changes in Lawrence's own life. From being an unknown provincial schoolmaster, who disliked his job, was dominated by his mother, and frustrated by his girl-friends, he very soon became the lover and husband of a remarkable aristocratic German woman, a man accepted as one of the leading young writers of his day and a well-known figure in the social life of the literary-philosophical intelligentsia. Many of the people from that world appear in various guises in *Women in Love*: Bertrand Russell as Sir Joshua, the sociologist; Lady Ottoline Morrell, the famous hostess, as Hermione; while the Café Royal set supplied the material for the bohemian London scenes, and Middleton Murry and Katherine Mansfield suggested some of the traits of Gerald and Gudrun. (Certainly in real life Lawrence tried to achieve the same sort of "blood-brotherhood" with Murry that Birkin wanted with Gerald—and with the same result.)

Across this rich and varied life fell the shadow of the Great War, a war that is not mentioned in *Women in Love*. Although the book was written in the middle of it and not published until 1921, it is still the world of before 1914 that is being described. But the despair to which the War drove Lawrence is surely reflected in the sense of exposed nerves, violence, cruelty, and death that pervades the book. It is Lawrence's most powerful work, but also his least relaxed and lyrical.

Frieda said that the War crushed Lawrence's "belief in

human civilisation." It was not so much the violence that shattered Lawrence (he was never a pacifist like Russell or many of the other young artists and intellectuals that he knew). Nor was it the suffering, of which he saw nothing himself—as he was physically unfit to serve in the forces. What horrified him was the regimentation—individual man being submerged in a vast, uniform, mechanical mass. Industrialism had already gone a long way towards doing this, helped by so-called "education," but the War had made the process complete. Private man in his individual human dignity had been abolished. Or where he survived, as Lawrence himself did, he was isolated and jeered at, and his work suppressed. (*The Rainbow* had been prosecuted, condemned, and destroyed on its first appearance in 1915.)

Lawrence loved his fellow men and wanted to help them by his writing. The thought of estrangement from them was cruel, but the problem of finding a true connexion with them was one he could not solve. He had achieved a lasting marriage, but he had failed to achieve the perfect conjunction with another man that he had hoped for, and he had failed to achieve a relationship with society as a whole. Moreover, his great love for England began to turn bitter during the war. He made several abortive attempts to escape to America, where he planned to found, with a few friends, a new community called Rananim, "which shall start a new life amongst us—a life in which the only riches is integrity of character. So that each one may fulfil his own nature and deep desires to the utmost, but wherein too, the ultimate satisfaction and joy is in the completeness of us all as one."

Nothing ever came of these efforts, and from what one knows of Lawrence's character it seems almost certain that such a community would have been doomed to failure. But they do suggest the change in Lawrence's preoccupations that took place during the War. His early life and books were dominated by sexual and family relationships, but his interests now shift to travel, to the search for a simpler and more natural life, to the problem of man's place amongst his fellow men, to political and religious man. These are the themes of most of his later novels.

REFERENCES

1. *W.L.*, p. 5.
2. *W.L.*, p. 365.
3. *W.L.*, p. 9.
4. *W.L.*, p. 15.
5. *W.L.*, p. 28.
6. *W.L.*, p. 10.
7. *W.L.*, p. 11.
8. *W.L.*, p. 77.
9. *W.L.*, p. 76.
10. *W.L.*, p. 78.
11. *W.L.*, p. 101.
12. *W.L.*, p. 223.
13. *W.L.*, p. 337.
14. *W.L.*, p. 122.
15. *W.L.*, p. 139.
16. *W.L.*, p. 283.
17. *W.L.*, pp. 293-4.
18. *W.L.*, p. 139.
19. *W.L.*, p. 191.
20. *W.L.*, p. 191.
21. *W.L.*, p. 198.
22. *W.L.*, p. 265.
23. *W.L.*, p. 242.
24. *W.L.*, p. 244.
25. *W.L.*, p. 247.
26. *W.L.*, p. 258.
27. *W.L.*, p. 301.
28. *W.L.*, p. 302.
29. *W.L.*, p. 306.
30. *W.L.*, p. 173.
31. *W.L.*, p. 143.
32. *W.L.*, p. 306.
33. *W.L.*, p. 347.
34. *W.L.*, p. 190.
35. *W.L.*, p. 366.
36. *W.L.*, p. 364.
37. *W.L.*, p. 407.
38. *W.L.*, p. 421.
39. *W.L.*, p. 434.
40. *W.L.*, p. 435.
41. *W.L.*, p. 463.
42. *W.L.*, p. 464.

CHAPTER IV

THE NOVELS OF TRAVEL

"Comes over one an absolute necessity to move." So begins *Sea and Sardinia*, the travel book published in the same year as *Women in Love*; and the phrase typifies Lawrence's own feelings immediately after the War. He felt that he had finished with England; the years of wandering lay ahead. Just as the Brangwen family's move to Beldover at the end of *The Rainbow* presaged the changed mood of *Women in Love*, so did the dramatic shift of scene to Austria at the end of that book strike a note that was to persist in the future books: all the subsequent novels (with the exception of *Lady Chatterley's Lover*) are set partly or wholly outside England. His travel books, poems and letters reflect his constantly changing surroundings. Perhaps one reason why he never again achieved the high quality of *Women in Love* was that his "flitting" (to use a chapter title from that book) did not allow him the mental concentration such a work demands. In one way or another all the later novels (again excepting *Lady Chatterley's Lover*) have to a greater or lesser degree an element of reportage about them, a documentary interest in life in Italy or Australia or Mexico, and many of the minor characters in them are malicious portraits of the men and women he met in those places.

The Lost Girl, the next novel after *Women in Love*, is something of a sport, in every sense of the word. Lawrence began it before the War and described it as "quite unlike my usual style." Lawrence had no doubt begun to realise that his serious novels would not command a wide sale, and he seems to have set out to make money by writing a more popular novel in the style of Bennett or Wells. However, when war broke out, the unfinished manuscript was in Germany, and Lawrence could not recover it until 1919. He then promptly rewrote it with an ending inspired by his own first post-war journey to Italy.

"It is meant to be comic—but not satire," Lawrence said, and the early part of the book is indeed comic—in places, even facetious—with "characters" in the main tradition of the English novel:

> By his side, somewhat tight and tubby, with his chest out and his head back, went the prim figure of Mr. May, reminding one of a consequential bird of the smaller species. His plumbago-grey suit fitted exactly —save that it was perhaps a little tight. The jacket and waistcoat were bound with silk braid of exactly the same shade as the cloth. His soft collar, immaculately fresh, had a dark stripe like his shirt. His boots were black, with grey suède uppers: but a *little* down at heel. His dark grey hat was jaunty. Altogether he looked very spruce, though a *little* behind the fashions: very pink-faced, though his blue eyes were bilious beneath: very much on the spot, although the spot was the wrong one.[1]

Also in the main tradition is the setting of the novel amongst the shopkeeper class, where material things are all-important, where the greatest disgrace is bankruptcy, and where old maids seem more numerous than wives. In fact one gets the feeling that Lawrence went out of his way in this book to do all the conventional things that he had forsworn in *The Rainbow* and *Women in Love*, just to show that he could do them as well as any other novelist, and that if he did not usually do them, this was by choice and not through lack of ability.

For the third time, he uses his native Eastwood as background. In *Sons and Lovers* it had been seen as a place full of individual working men and women; in *Women in Love* the common people had become an anonymous mass and it was the tiny local aristocracy of wealth, power and education who were in the foreground; in *The Lost Girl* the quite different world of the middle class is presented. Any one of these three pictures would, in itself, have justified our calling Lawrence a penetrating sociological novelist, but the sureness of touch displayed throughout this whole triptych reveals a range of social comprehension unsurpassed in twentieth-century English fiction.

The story is about Alvina Houghton, who seems condemned to the stuffiest sort of feminine bourgeois existence. Her father is the big local draper, proprietor of Manchester House, who feels it his mission to introduce the latest fashions and fabrics to the little mining town. The miners' wives will have none of it, of course; James Houghton's good taste is wasted on them. His decline is both comic and pathetic. One "Great Bargain Event" follows another, prices are cut and cut again, the fashionable materials are at last bought up for children's underwear ("Yah-h-h, yer've got Houghton's threp'ny draws on!" cry the local schoolgirls). The foursquare shop that had dominated the little town dwindles away; parts are let off and eventually Mr Houghton has to give away the remains of his stock. Always a speculator, he tries investing in a brick-field, then in a small coalmine of his own, and last of all in "The Pleasure Palace," a ramshackle hall in the next village that he runs as a cinema-cum-theatre.

While Mr Houghton plays with and loses his money, the women around him wither away. His wife suffers from a weak heart and dies after a married life of semi-invalidism, and the establishment is left to Miss Frost (symbolic name) the governess, an admirable and upright lady who keeps the home together, and Miss Pinnegar, very much a class below Miss Frost, who runs the shop and supervises the work-girls.

Alvina, determined to make something of her life,

decides to become a midwife. A resolute, unprudish and competent girl, she goes to a sordid training-home in London, and thrives on the round of slum births. She returns home to find that none of the locals will pay for her maternity services—and relapses into the old dark house and dreary way of life.

The opening of the Pleasure Palace promises Alvina a new life, though it is regarded as something of a social come-down that she should play the piano there. At least there is novelty in the world of Mr May, the effeminate, down-at-heel impresario, and of the visiting acting troupes (who are in the long tradition of itinerant performers that stretches back through Dickens to the days of Fielding). Yet they are literally at the end of that tradition, for at the Pleasure Palace they only fill in the gaps between the films. One of the minor themes of the book is the way in which the cinema is killing the old live theatre, and making people prefer the mechanical to life and imagination. It is an unexpected theme for Lawrence, though it obviously connects with his general condemnation of modern civilisation.

One of the visiting troupes is the Natcha-Kee-Tawaras —Madame and her four young men (two Swiss, one French, and one Italian) with their famed Red Indian act. The atmosphere of the group is somewhat unhealthy, with an absurdly theatrical-chivalric worship by the young men of Madame, the mother-figure who looks after them. But it is the Italian, Cicio, who fascinates Alvina. He is not a noble savage; like the other performers he is commonplace and not particularly intelligent, certainly not noble. But there is something "mindless and intent" about him: and at the appearance of this so Lawrencian phrase in this hitherto un-Lawrencian novel, the reader may well surmise that Alvina's goose is cooked. Yet she does not submit at once: she still feels that her present existence is "life itself," although it so obviously is not:

They *were* unreal, Madame and Cicio and the rest. Cicio was just a fantasy blown in on the wind, to blow away again. The real, permanent thing was Woodhouse, the *semper idem* Knarborough Road, and the unchangeable grubby gloom of Manchester House, with the stuffy, padding Miss Pinnegar, and her father, whose fingers, whose very soul seemed dirty with pennies. These were the solid permanent fact. These were life itself. And Cicio, splashing up on his bay horse and green cloth, he was a mountebank and an extraneous nonentity, a coloured old rag blown down the Knarborough Road into Limbo. Into Limbo. Whilst Miss Pinnegar and her father sat frowstily on for ever, eating their toast and cutting off the crust and sipping their third cup of tea.[2]

At last she rebels—after all, she is thirty—and leaves home to join the troupe: " 'You're a lost girl!', cried Miss Pinnegar. . . . 'I like being lost,' said Alvina."[3] But she sickens of the troupe, and they sicken of her; and when they are in Lancaster, she applies for and gets a job as a midwife. The Natcha-Kee-Tawaras were vivid after life at home, but now, following weeks of life with them in theatrical digs, she welcomes the cleanliness and usefulness of life in hospital, tea with the matron and the local ladies. She grows fat and jolly once more. This part of the story is again totally different from anything else that Lawrence wrote: it has the air of a superior woman's serial, right down to the middle-aged Scots bachelor doctor, who has a Georgian teapot and Queen Anne teacups and proposes to Alvina in the attic of his "pleasant old square house."

Alvina wants marriage, but not him. However, it is August 1914 and the war is an excuse for delay. Then Cicio arrives in the town (the troupe having disbanded), and as Alvina is waiting to deliver a patient's baby he appears to serenade her at the house, dying for her love.

As the patient remarks: " 'I'm howling with one sort of pain, he's howling with another'."[4]

Alvina marries Cicio and they make the long wartime journey to his home in the Abruzzi. A journey always excited Lawrence and brought out the best of his descriptive writing; Alvina's and Cicio's journey is one that Lawrence had made himself, and it is vividly rendered. Even more strikingly conveyed is what greets the couple on arrival—an utterly remote house in the mountains where they have to live with—and live like—animals. This is far from being the conventional picture of Italy: it is bitterly cold, the peasants are rancorous and dangerous, the rural slums are infinitely worse than in England, and the churches much uglier.

Soon Cicio is called up, and Alvina is left alone, pregnant. She is indeed a lost girl. One day, perhaps, Cicio will return, and then they may go to America. She loves him, she is his woman, and despite all the hardship that is better than being an old maid back in Nottinghamshire.

The Lost Girl stands alone amongst the novels, because it is the only one in which Lawrence is not, to a greater or lesser degree, propounding or working out his own problems. His deepest feelings and experiences are not engaged. But within the limits he set himself, it is a successful and enjoyable book.

In fact it is much more successful than Lawrence's next novel, *Aaron's Rod*, where his own presence is only too much felt. Setting *The Lost Girl* aside as at least partly a relic from a much earlier period of Lawrence's life, *Aaron's Rod* comes immediately after the two masterpieces, *The Rainbow* and *Women in Love*. But if one has expectations of another work of the same high order, they are to be bitterly disappointed by this book.

Lawrence says here nothing that he did not say better elsewhere. What is profound in *Women in Love* here becomes superficial or even silly and the tough verbal battles of that book degenerate into nagging or boring tirades. Much of the novel is in fact at the level of journalism; parts of it, indeed, might be direct transcripts of those pieces that Lawrence wrote "in an hour and a half" for the *Evening News* and *Sunday Dispatch* (and which were reprinted in *Assorted Articles*). It is significant that an early chapter of the book is called "Talk," and the final one "Words." Towards the end of "Talk" we have: " 'Good-bye,' said Tanny. 'I've been awfully bored'." The reader may well echo the remark. Unfortunately, Tanny (the Frieda figure in this book) is packed off for most of the rest of the action, and the book certainly suffers from the loss of her common sense and criticism.

Superficially, the novel traces a course parallel to that of *The Lost Girl*. Alvina leaves the narrow life of Eastwood for Italy and a new world at the very beginning of the War; this book starts on the first Christmas Eve after the War with Aaron Sisson walking out on his wife and two children. He is a checkweighman, secretary of his Miners' Union, and looked upon as a man of peculiar understanding by the miners. Although trained to be a teacher, and able to play the flute and piccolo to professional standard, he prefers the mine. On Christmas Eve he goes out to have a drink and to buy candles for the children's tree—and does not return. His wife calls him selfish, and it is hard to find any answer to this charge. Nor does Aaron give any very convincing reason for going. He is just angry with everything and feels imprisoned after twelve years of marriage: "I like being by myself—I hate feeling and caring, and being forced into it. I want to be left alone."[5]

Aaron goes to London and becomes a flautist in the Covent Garden orchestra. There he meets Lilly, the Lawrence figure of the novel. (One can tell the Lawrence figure in any of his books by the fact that he is nearly always called by his surname, as Lawrence was in life, *e.g.* Birkin, Lilly, Somers, even Mellors. After *Sons and Lovers*, Lawrence stopped being "Bert," and his self-portraits also stop using Christian names.) Tanny, Lilly's wife, has gone back to visit her people in Norway, just as Frieda returned to Germany after the War. Lilly "had a certain belief in himself as a saviour."[6] Left alone in a flat in Covent Garden, he sees Aaron ill in the street, takes him in and nurses him through the subsequent illness, which is apparently the direct result of being seduced by a young woman. Considering that Aaron had just brutally abandoned his wife and children, his account of the affair is rather odd:

> "I gave in to her—and afterwards I cried, thinking of Lottie and the children. I felt my heart break, you know. And that's what did it. I should have been all right if I hadn't given in to her."[7]

Lilly, like his original, is an admirable cook, housewife, darner of socks and tender of the sick. He obviously relishes his authority over the sick man, who behaves with a "dim kind of obedience." Lilly-Lawrence without Tanny-Frieda is enjoying himself. "The fool would die, without me," he meditates. "As soon as this man's really better he'll punch me in the wind, metaphorically if not actually, for having interfered with him. And Tanny would say he was quite right to do it. She says I want power over them. . . . Why can't they submit to a bit of healthy authority?"[8] One wishes that Tanny-Frieda *were* there, for it might save a lot of self-pity and self-deception on the part of Lilly-Lawrence. As it is, we are treated to page after page of tiresome and abusive generalisations about women, and about children, and about women again.

These tirades recur throughout the book, in the mouths of various characters, until one is thoroughly tired of men rambling on so pathetically and impotently about being henpecked, bullied, and generally humiliated by women. There is not, I think, a single satisfactory sexual relationship—not even a single satisfactory sexual encounter—in the whole book. So it is not surprising that the idea of men sticking together is again produced, though it is evident by now that the idea of an equal brotherhood (as with Birkin and Gerald) has given way to that of one man in authority and another in obedience to him.

The lack of women is very noticeable. In all Lawrence's other books at least one woman plays a leading part; in *Aaron's Rod*, the few women that appear are faint shadows (once Tanny has made her few memorable remarks and departed). Indeed the book might well be called "Men without Women"; but just as Lawrence could not do without women in real life, the attempt to do so in his fiction is also a failure.

Lilly feels the urge to go abroad—to Malta and on to Italy. Aaron asks, what is the good? "You'll be the same there as you are here." Curiously enough, Lilly "had not expected this criticism," but eventually manages to reply that "a new place brings out a new thing in a man."[9] Lilly goes, and some months later writes inviting Aaron to join him. There is some acute social observation, not altogether unkind, of Englishmen (and one or two women) in Italy: "Why is it, do you think, that English people abroad go so very *queer*—so ultra-English —*incredible*!—and at the same time so perfectly impossible?"[10] Most of these figures have been identified with people Lawrence met in Florence and elsewhere, particularly Norman Douglas, who appears as Argyle. Aaron finds the Italian landscape and people expansive after "the cosy English ambushed life," and amongst the statues of the Piazza della Signoria in Florence he has a sense of arriving "at the perfect centre of the human world." This is before his letter-case has been stolen by a gang of Italian soldiers, before he is blown up and his precious flute destroyed in a bomb outrage in a café, before he has seen violence between political demonstrators and the police.

However, the only real incident of the Florence section is Aaron's passion for the American-born wife of the Italian Marchese del Torre. She sings, and when Aaron accompanies her on the flute "for the first time her soul drew its own deep breath."[11] They sleep together, and Aaron immediately decides, "this is not my woman." He feels "blasted" by her "strange and hateful power." However, a week later he is sleeping with her again. He again discovers that "he disliked her. Or if not her, then her whole motive. Her whole life-mode."[12] After that he can only return to Lilly: he decides that if he has got to give in to someone, it had better be to Lilly, "rather than to the quicksands of woman or the stinking bog of society."[13] It is all excellent wish-fulfilment on Lawrence's part. In the realm of fiction, at least, he has the prospect of one obedient disciple.

Some of the weakness of the novel lies in the character of the nominal hero, Aaron. It seems likely that Lawrence did conceive of him originally as a sort of male Alvina Houghton. However, this aesthetic, working-class refugee from Eastwood, making his way through the bohemian world of London to the social world of Florence, is too close to Lawrence's own character, without being Lawrence. Possibly Lawrence, in a mood of dissatisfaction with his marriage, thought he might project this dissatisfaction artistically in the figure of Aaron, but the moment Lawrence himself enters the action, as Lilly, Aaron is doomed to take second place. To move with the apparent ease that Aaron does in all sorts of different social milieux needed someone with Lawrence's own peculiar gifts and genius, but it is made embarrassingly clear that Aaron does not possess these qualities. (All he has is his flute—the "Rod" of the book's title.) Thus, after one long passage purporting to give Aaron's thoughts on women ("her will, her will, her terrible, implacable, cunning will!" etc. etc.), we have:

Don't grumble at me then, gentle reader, and swear at me that this damned fellow wasn't half clever enough to think all these smart things, and realise all these fine-drawn-out subtleties. You are quite right, he wasn't, yet it all resolved itself in him as I say, and it is for you to prove that it didn't.[14]

Such a paragraph would have been utterly unthinkable in *Women in Love* or *The Rainbow*, or indeed in the earlier novels. It is symptomatic of the artistic incoherence of the book's construction and of the rather jaunty tone that makes parts of it so inferior even to most of Lawrence's journalism. The action is almost non-existent, and there is altogether too much talk and verbiage without the wonderful concrete realisation of the inward action that we have in *Women in Love*. Above all, there is no real conflict: Aaron's likeness to Lilly-Lawrence, the lack of self-criticism, and the absence of women characters ensure this.

In the next novel, *Kangaroo*, the setting is Australia. Frieda is with Lawrence again and the two appear practically undisguised as the Somers and Harriet of the novel. There is an autumnal aura about their marriage: sex is quiescent and we are even informed that they occupy separate bedrooms. Tribute is paid to Harriet's "gay, undying courage, her wonderful fresh zest in front of life";[15] but there is some bitter argument between the two, centring on the man's need for some relation with other people, beyond marriage.

One is made to realise how desperately isolated Somers-Lawrence is in the world: he is set apart from his fellow men, a wanderer on the face of the earth with no job, no children, and no place in society. All he has is his wife, and he "knew that her greatest grief was when he turned away from their personal human life of intimacy to this impersonal business of male activity for which he was always craving."[16] He has a terrible dream in which the two people he had loved—his wife and mother—combine into one woman who accuses him of betraying her love for him. They had both believed in him terribly, in personal being. "But in the impersonal man, a man that would go beyond them, with his back to them, away from them into an activity that excluded them, in this man they did not find it so easy to believe."[17]

But Somers-Lawrence desperately needs this further life:

"I want to do something with living people, some-where, somehow, while I live on the earth. I write, but I write alone. And I live alone. Without any connec-tion whatever with the rest of men."[18]

Harriet retorts that his writing is enough "doing." She is scornful of his other aspirations. She knows that he will only be disappointed in his efforts for mankind, and then turn back again to her. In his heart of hearts Somers knows she is right, but he still feels the desire to be a leader, to make one final attempt to influence men by action.

Somers is a much more attractive person than Lilly. The strident and rather ridiculous figure in *Aaron's Rod* is here replaced by an odd and appealing, sometimes al-most pathetic, little man (his littleness is emphasised) who possesses some of "the magic of the old world . . . the old culture, the old glamour."[19]

"A comical-looking bloke! Perhaps a Bolshie." So a Sydney workman describes him on the first page of the novel, and the remark sheds light both on Somers and on Australians. To Lawrence a new country is always far more than just the scenery, wonderfully though he will render that: it is the feel of the place, above all the way the people live, that interests him. The Australian am-bience is powerfully invoked and dramatically presented from the very first paragraph of the book: the lack of subtlety, the free and easy casualness which ends either in profound indifference or in sheer take-it-or-leave-it "bloody-mindedness." In this relaxed atmosphere the Somerses settle in at their suburban bungalow and gradually become friendly with the couple next door, Jack and Victoria Calcott. There is some lively description of middle-class suburban life. Jack tells Somers of the movement in which he is involved—an organisation of ex-servicemen's clubs, the "Diggers," ostensibly social and athletic, but secretly organised on semi-military lines, aiming at revolution and the seizure of power. The head of the movement is a Jewish lawyer in Sydney, known as Kangaroo.

Kangaroo is one of Lawrence's most ambitious attempts at creating a male character who is not at all like Lawrence himself. We know that no such man and no such political movement existed in Australia at the time. Both were invented by Lawrence as dramatisations of the sort of political leader and movement with which he might usefully work. One cannot imagine him participating in the traditional English political system, nor indeed can one see him giving his whole-hearted allegience to any conventional established party. The Diggers' movement is rather contrived; as far as one can see, their only reason for wanting a revolution is that they crave excitement and "are dying for another scrap." Kangaroo himself is unlike any obvious dictator, and his idea of the new society that the revolution will bring about is extremely sketchy—a sort of wise and benevolent despotism. But the man is powerfully presented, alternatively grotesque and beautiful, loving and ferocious: in him Lawrence creates the strong opponent-friend for his hero that was so lacking in *Aaron's Rod*.

The personal love-hate relationship between Somers and Kangaroo is dramatically worked out. But Somers-Lawrence is not really concerned any more with the idea of conjunction between two men; and while he is interested in the possibility of political action changing the present, he is sceptical about its effect on the future:

"Sometimes I feel I'd give anything, soul and body, for a smash-up in this social-industrial world we're in. And I would. And then when I realise people—just people—the same people after it as before—why then I don't care any more, and feel it's time to turn to the gods."[20]

The last phrase reveals the new interest that is now growing in Lawrence—no longer women, no longer men, no longer political power—but "the gods". For the time being, however, he is still sufficiently fascinated by politics to extend Somers' experiences to include the socialist rivals of Kangaroo's faction. He meets Willie Struthers, a labour leader, who wants to enlist his services and offers him the editorship of a socialist paper. Somers is "touched on one of his quivering strings" by Struthers' appeal to his working-class feelings, the appeal to the "love of a man for his mate." But he rejects it: absolute love for "a mate" would be as fatal as absolute love for a woman: "When human love starts out to lock individuals together, it is just courting disaster."[21]

He leaves Struthers to go straight to Kangaroo and tell him much the same thing: "Don't love me. Don't want me to love you. Let's be hard separate men."[22] At this, Kangaroo becomes hideous and malignant, threatens Somers and orders him to leave the country. Somers, absolutely terrified, with Kangaroo following "slowly, awfully, behind, like a mad man," manages to escape from the house, and walks out into the Sydney streets in fear.

The story has moved forward with reasonable momentum through two hundred pages to this climax of terror. The atmosphere of conspiracy and fear and malignity around the rival leaders is conveyed with some of the force found in Conrad's political novels. Lawrence has built up a situation of physical excitement, rare in his novels. What will happen to Somers? Will he be killed?

or driven out of the country? We turn expectantly to the next chapter, "The Nightmare," and find—total collapse.

For the next fifty pages the story is forgotten, and Australia is not even mentioned. Instead, we are given pure Lawrencian autobiography—more direct and circumstantial than in *Sons and Lovers*—with nothing changed but the people's names. It is an account of Frieda's and Lawrence's life during the 1914–18 War. Lawrence did not mention the War in the novels which he wrote when it was actually in progress, but now, three or four years after it had ended, he feels an overwhelming need to let out the pent-up feelings that it aroused in him. So, ironically, in this Australian fiction, the most violent emotions presented are those actually experienced in wartime England by Lawrence himself, "one of the most intensely English little men England ever produced."[23]

As we have seen, what really shocked Lawrence about the War was not the tragic waste, the horror and futility of the carnage; it was what he regarded as the invasion of his privacy, the desire of the authorities to "humiliate him as a separate, single man. . . ." The following passage is symptomatic:

Oh, foul dogs. But they were very close on him now, very close. They were grinning very close behind him, like hyenas just going to bite. Yes, they were running him to earth. They had exposed all his nakedness to gibes. And they were pining, almost whimpering to give the last grab at him, and haul him to earth, a victim. Finished! But not yet! Oh, no, not yet. Not yet, not now, nor ever. Not while life was life, should they lay hold of him. Never again. Never would he be touched again. And because they had handled his private parts, and looked into them, their eyes should burst and their hands should wither and their hearts should rot. So he cursed them in his blood, with an unremitting curse, as he waited.[24]

This outburst was occasioned by a perfectly routine medical examination which Lawrence had (in common with every other man of military age in the country) to see if he were fit for service. This hysterical fury illustrates in an extreme form the central passion in Lawrence's life, *the desire to be left alone*.

He had, in fact, a great deal to be bitter about during the War—ill-health, dire poverty, the banning of *The Rainbow*, and subsequent difficulty in getting his other work published. All this he bore with stoicism and courage. Yet he went half-crazy about a medical examination and about an imagined persecution campaign on a vast scale to bring him to "the heel of a Jewish financier." One may feel that this does no credit to his intelligence. He himself admits that it was "irrational," but "there is no arguing with the instinctive passional self."[25]

It has been claimed that this long autobiographical diversion is an integral part of the structure of the novel, because it sheds light on Somers-Lawrence's thoughts and feelings about society and politics. Obviously there is a continuum between Lawrence in wartime England and Lawrence in Australia a few years later; but if all that was required was to give some background depth to the present Somers, Lawrence could have done this in a few pages (as he gave the background of Gerald Crich in *Women in Love*) without disrupting the story at its most critical part. But quite obviously Lawrence is here in the grip of a compulsive need to retell this nightmare experience in his past—and the strength of the need may be judged from the difficulty he finds in getting back to his story.

Even when he has worked finally through the war experiences and their effect on him, there is a chapter called "Bits" which consists literally of bits from the Sydney *Bulletin*, interspersed with bits of scenery and bits of preaching. "This gramophone of a novel," he calls it;

and a page or two later we are back to "dear reader" stuff (in the worst style of *Aaron's Rod*), while the next chapter begins: "Chapter follows chapter and nothing doing." By this time seventy pages have passed since we left Somers walking the Sydney streets in fear after the escape from Kangaroo. The impetus of the story has been completely lost; but it comes to life again for one dramatic episode. There is a great Labour rally in Sydney that Somers attends; as Willie Struthers addresses it, a riot organised by Kangaroo's Diggers breaks out. Shots are fired, a bomb is thrown—and Kangaroo is mortally wounded. On his deathbed he pleads with Somers to tell him that he loves him, but Somers cannot bring himself to tell this lie. So Kangaroo dies in the prime of life, fulfilled neither through his political aims nor through his love for Somers.

It is also the end of Somers-Lawrence's dream of action and leadership in the world of men. However important the world of men and the great human loves for wife, child or comrade, "something else was true at the same time. Man's isolation was always a supreme truth and fact, not to be forsworn. And the mystery of apartness. And the greater mystery of the dark God beyond a man. . . ."[26]

Despite the disruption of the story, there is a coherent progression of thought and belief throughout the book. Lawrence begins with the need for some connexion with the world of men—the old dream of the artist to be a man of action—and finds this ambition running counter to the wife's demand for a purely personal life. Then comes the realisation that political action is useless because, although it may change events, it does not change men; then re-affirmation of the supreme importance of the individual; and, lastly, the newly-expressed belief in the "dark gods." Lawrence does little to define the dark gods. They are "forever unrealisable," their medium is the profound unconscious, and they are the complete antithesis of the spiritual-ideal, possessively loving God of Christianity, who is a "proposition of the mental consciousness."

Australia acts as a counterpoint to these main themes. As ever, Lawrence's feelings for a new place have all the fluctuations and contradictions of his feelings for another person. So, when he first arrives in Sydney, we find him, rather incredibly, pining for London Bridge, St Martin's Lane and Westminster. But by the end of the book he is rejecting Europe and its "huge ponderous cathedrals and factories and cities," and loving the "uncreatedness" of the Australian landscape, both man-made and natural:

Since that day he had been thankful for the amorphous scrappy scattering of foundationless shacks and bungalows. Since then he had loved the Australian landscape, with the remote gum trees running their white nerves into the air, the random streets of flimsy bungalows, all loose from one another, and temporary seeming, the bungalows perched precariously on the knolls, like Japanese paper-houses, below the ridge of wire-and-tuft trees . . . the flimsy hills of Australia were like a new world, and the frail *inconspicuousness* of the landscape, that was still so clear and clean, clean of all fogginess or confusion: but the frail, aloof, inconspicuous clarity of the landscape was like a sort of heaven—bungalows, shacks, corrugated iron and all.[27]

Kangaroo contains some of Lawrence's most brilliant natural description—pictures of small towns, of Sydney Harbour, of the Pacific coast, of the bush, and of the onset of an Australian spring. These have a freshness and lyricism reminiscent of *The White Peacock*, but at the same time all the power of Lawrence's mature art. Yet, despite his delight in the beauty of Australia, the "absolute necessity to move" is on Somers-Lawrence again; and the book ends with him (and Harriet-Frieda) sailing for America, "which seemed to lie next in his line of destiny."

There was no very potent reason why the political theme of *Kangaroo* should have been set in Australia; it was more or less accidental that a certain phase of Lawrence's feelings and interests should coincide with his stay there. But in *The Plumed Serpent*, his next novel, the setting is inseparable from the spiritual action. A passage from Lawrence's essay "New Mexico" makes the point:

I had looked over all the world for something that would strike *me* as religious. The simple piety of some English people, the semi-pagan mystery of some Catholics in southern Italy, the intensity of some Bavarian peasants, the semi-ecstasy of Buddhists or Brahmins: all this had seemed religious all right, as far as the parties concerned were involved, but it didn't involve me. . . . I had no permanent feeling of religion till I came to New Mexico and penetrated into the old human race-experience there.[28]

In *Kangaroo* the dark gods had been symbols. In *The Plumed Serpent* Lawrence attempts to make them manifest. It is a major undertaking; and he himself called the book "my most important novel, so far." Whatever our own judgment of the book's importance, it is obvious that Lawrence intended it as a more significant work than his last three novels. He must have realised that *The Lost Girl*, *Aaron's Rod* and *Kangaroo* were, in their various ways, minor works compared with *The Rainbow* and *Women in Love*, and have felt the ambition to create another major work to stand beside those masterpieces.

The first thing he did was to remove the Lawrence figure from amongst the characters, and to leave the centre of the stage to Kate Leslie, an Irish widow of forty. She has had two husbands, and her children are grown-up. She no longer wants love or excitement or "the thing called 'Life' "; she wants "to be alone with the unfolding flower of her own soul, in the delicate chiming silence that is at the midst of things."[29]

The novel opens with Kate and two American male companions going to a bullfight in Mexico City. The fight is cheap, cruel and ugly, and Kate leaves in disgust; but the Americans are convinced that this "was seeing LIFE, and what can an American do more!" This sort of "life" is, of course, exactly what Kate is trying to escape. So is the "life" represented by the social gatherings of English and American expatriates with their endless bickerings. She wants to get away from these and from Mexico City itself, with its "underlying ugliness, a sort of squalid evil, which made Naples seem debonair in comparison."[30]

One day in a newspaper she sees an item headed "The Gods of Antiquity Return to Mexico." It reports how a man of great stature had been seen to rise naked from the Lake of Sayula (in the distant interior of the country) and walk to the shore, where he had assured the astonished peasants that the old gods were about to return to them— in particular Quetzalcoatl (the "Plumed Serpent" of the title). Kate, who has felt little but bitterness in Mexico so far, finds in this curious piece of news "a strange beam of wonder and mystery, almost like hope." By chance she has already met Don Ramón, a man of almost pure Spanish descent, who has an estate beside the Lake of Sayula. He and his friend Don Cipriano, a general in the army, of pure Indian descent, are to be the two main male characters in the book.

Kate Leslie sets off for the Lake, and her journey there (Chapter Four of the novel) is one of Lawrence's finest pieces of writing. It is far more than brilliant travel writing (though it is that); it is an evocation of the "delicate, tender mystery" of this unknown faith. In a superb scene, Kate is ferried by a crippled boatman across the waters of the Lake that is the Galilee of the new religion, and has her boat stopped by a beautiful Indian who walks out to it and announces: "I am Quetzalcoatl's man, I."

Kate takes a house in the town of Sayula and a realistic strain now accompanies the mysterious one, as in this view of the sacred lake:

Lumps of women were by the water's edge. Westwards, down the glare, rose the broken-looking villas and the white twin towers of the church, holding up its two fingers in mockery above the scarlet flame trees and the dark mangoes. She saw the rather lousy shore, and smelt the smell of Mexico, come out in the hot sun after the rains: excrement, human and animal, dried in the sun on a dry, dry earth; and dry leaves; and mango leaves; and pure air with a little refuse-smoke in it.[31]

Realistic, too, is the description of the surrounding country—half-wild, murderous, full of bandits—and of the rather faded little town itself, superficially aping European or American "civilisation," but basically reverting to a more primitive life. This is dramatically conveyed in the Saturday-night scene in the Plaza. The flappers and young men of the district come in by motor car, and rather forlornly parade around in their best clothes and gyrate to the jazz band. But, as the evening wears on, their music is obliterated by the sound of a tom-tom and a flute, which proclaim the "timeless, primeval passion of the prehistoric races, with their intense and complicated religious significance."[32] Then an old man preaches and a hymn is sung, both of them announcing the death of Jesus and the coming of Quetzalcoatl. Then men and women start a long wheeling dance. Kate, who has been watching, joins in, and feels herself transported into a new life "of greater womanhood." Quite what this means one does not know, though it is obviously a sort of rebirth, such as she was hoping for when she first decided to journey to Sayula. Although it is presumably chiefly a spiritual state, it is induced by sensuous means: indeed it gains credibility from the fact that it comes at the end of such a vividly realistic and concrete piece of description.

The replacement of Christianity by the new-old religion gathers momentum. It becomes clear that Don Ramón is the living representative (if not the actual incarnation) of Quetzalcoatl—standing for the sensual fulfilment of the soul. His wife, Dona Carlota, a devout and extremely spiritual Christian, represents the faith that he wants to replace. The fight between them is to the death. The rebirth of Quetzalcoatl brings rebirth to Kate, but the death of Christianity brings literally death to Dona Carlota. She dies after making her violent protest in the church of Sayula, from which all the Christian images have been removed and burnt, and which is now being reconsecrated to Quetzalcoatl by her husband. Kate watches the dying agony of this woman, who belongs to the same civilisation as she does, but with no sign of sorrow or pity.

For Kate is absorbed not only by the religion, but also by the primeval magic of Don Cipriano, Ramón's chief disciple: "she wanted to be covered with deep and living darkness, the deeps where Cipriano could lay her."[33] And —although she has her moments of wanting to go home, back to simple human people—Kate herself

> had convinced herself of one thing, finally: that the clue to all living and to all moving-on into new living lay in the vivid blood-relation between man and woman. A man and a woman in this togetherness were the clue to all present living and future possibility. Out of this clue of togetherness between a man and a woman, the whole of the new life arose. It was the quick of the whole.[34]

This relationship she has at last found with Cipriano, and she is married to him by Ramón according to the rites of Quetzalcoatl. Cipriano's love makes "all her body flower": with him she finds complete sexual fulfilment.

Yet she still hankers after her old liberty to move around the world—until she thinks with horror of the sort of life women of her own age lead back in "civilisation":

Another thing, she had observed, with a touch of horror. One after the other, her women "friends," the powerful love-women, at the age of forty, forty-five, fifty, they lost all their charm and allure, and turned into real grimalkins, greyish, avid, and horrifying, prowling around looking for prey that became scarcer and scarcer. As human beings they went to pieces. And they remained these grey-ribbed grimalkins, dressed in elegant clothes, the grimalkin howl even passing into their smart chatter.[35]

The book ends with Kate in very much the same position as Alvina Houghton at the end of *The Lost Girl*—married to a strange and "mindless" man, in an alien land; and if neither woman is completely satisfied with her new life, both are convinced that it is infinitely preferable to the alternative of growing old alone in a narrow society at home. One might push the parallel further and say that there seems at times little to choose between the pseudo-Red-Indian Natcha-Kee-Tawaras nonsense in the earlier book and the Quetzalcoatl "high-flown bunk" (as Kate herself calls it) in this book.

Lawrence's attempt to create a new religion was inevitably doomed to failure. Novelists are not founders of religions. But the surprising thing is that he should have attempted to do so in such detail. For he constructed a complete liturgy, produced enough hymns to fill a small book, and elaborately described costumes and ceremonies. These are not so much ridiculous as boring—a monument to misused talent. Yet the most damning criticism of this religion-making is that Lawrence is going against his own deepest instincts by producing a mechanical and too conscious systematisation of what should have been intuitive and unconscious. The "dark gods" are intuitively felt in the depths of human psyche: by bringing them to the surface and cluttering them up with claptrap, Lawrence effectively kills them, leaving only a collection of images as tawdry as those thrown out of the church at Sayula when Christianity was expelled.

Kate's spiritual Odyssey—the main theme of the book —could have been just as effectively described without there being any church of Quetzalcoatl. Her two great experiences—in the dance and in her sexual love for Cipriano—need no established church. For at the end of the book the religion of Quetzalcoatl is, *by law*, made the national religion of the Mexican Republic. This is surely the final irony, the ultimate humiliation of the dark gods: that Lawrence, the supreme nonconformist, the passionate individualist who craved a religion in his deepest soul, should create a religion and then make it an established church by act of parliament! If only it had been left as the beautiful and delicate mystery that was first invoked on the Lake of Sayula or in the sensuous ecstasy of the dance in the plaza of the little town, the book would have been purged of a lot of dross. Perhaps it is not too much to see, in the fantastic elaboration of the church, Lawrence the frustrated leader and prophet trying to do in fiction what he was unable to do in life.

The theme of Kate and her coming to terms with middle age is a significant one. In some ways her entering of new circles of experience is akin to the spiritual developments which were described in *The Rainbow*, but there restricted to the young or at least fairly young. To make a widow his heroine is a reminder of Lawrence's own age: he celebrated his fortieth birthday soon after finishing *The Plumed Serpent*, in 1925, and Frieda was then already in her mid-forties. Even more significant is the fact that coming to terms with middle age is not in fact an acceptance of fading beauty and of living without love. On the contrary, for Kate it brings for the first time true recognition of the beauty and power of sex. Kate feels "life surging vivid and resistant within her":

"It is sex," she said to herself. "How wonderful sex can be, when men keep it powerful and sacred, and it fills the world! Like sunshine through and through one!..."[36]

Sex has played a very subordinate part in the last three novels, while Lawrence has been exploring man's relationships—not with women, but with his fellow men (both as individuals and as a community), and with God or "the gods." Yet, at the end of Lawrence's great attempt at a "religious" novel, we are left with this simple human fact of sexual love, pointing unmistakably forward to Lawrence's next (and final) novel, the "direct phallic book," *Lady Chatterley's Lover*.

REFERENCES

1. *L.G.*, p. 91.
2. *L.G.*, p. 149.
3. *L.G.*, p. 224.
4. *L.G.*, p. 288.
5. *A.R.*, p. 63.
6. *A.R.*, p. 67.
7. *A.R.*, p. 84.
8. *A.R.*, p. 91.
9. *A.R.*, p. 98.
10. *A.R.*, p. 210.
11. *A.R.*, p. 248.
12. *A.R.*, p. 265.
13. *A.R.*, p. 280.
14. *A.R.*, p. 161.
15. *K.*, p. 62.
16. *K.*, p. 93.
17. *K.*, p. 95.
18. *K.*, p. 66.
19. *K.*, p. 14.
20. *K.*, p. 162.
21. *K.*, p. 201.
22. *K.*, p. 213.
23. *K.*, p. 227.
24. *K.*, p. 261.
25. *K.*, p. 267.
26. *K.*, p. 334.
27. *K.*, p. 354.
28. *P.*, pp. 143-4.
29. *P.S.*, p. 54.
30. *P.S.*, p. 15.
31. *P.S.*, pp. 215–16.
32. *P.S.*, p. 113.
33. *P.S.*, p. 350.
34. *P.S.*, p. 397.
35. *P.S.*, p. 437.
36. *P.S.*, p. 434.

CHAPTER V

LADY CHATTERLEY'S LOVER

Lady Chatterley's Lover is undoubtedly the most generally known of Lawrence's books, but it owes its fame to its history of legal repression rather than to its intrinsic merits. For thirty-two years after its first publication (in Florence in 1928) the book was banned in England. This is not to say that it did not circulate: the eminence of its author and the reputation of its contents ensured a steady import of copies from the Continent secreted about the persons of returning travellers, and a consequent circulation amongst the universities, schools, clubs, and messes of the kingdom. Thus the authorities by their ban ensured that the book and its theme should be treated in exactly the way that Lawrence most deplored: the way that makes sex a furtive, forbidden, shameful matter of momentary titillation.

Lawrence's reputation grew steadily during this period, and simultaneously there was a great liberalisation in public discussion and writing about sexual matters. Symptomatic of this was the passing in 1959 of the Obscene Publications Act, the aim of which was not only to come down heavily on the obviously pornographic publication, but at the same time to provide safeguards for works of genuine literary, artistic or scientific merit that dealt with sex. In fact *Lady Chatterley's Lover* was exactly the sort of book that the original sponsors had in mind when drafting their act as being in need of protection from the indiscriminate rigours of the old law. It was ironic, therefore, that it should be the first novel to be prosecuted under the new act. The reasons behind this extraordinary action will probably never be known. The trial was spread over nearly a fortnight of October and November 1960, and for that period made the headlines in every paper from the most serious to the most popular, took up hours of time on radio and television, and became one of the chief topics of conversation throughout the country. On acquittal, Penguin Books could not keep pace with the demand for copies, and well over a million were sold within a few weeks. The Director of Public Prosecutions thus set in motion the biggest publicity campaign that any English novel has ever received.

The book marks a distinct break from Lawrence's previous three novels. *Aaron's Rod*, *Kangaroo* and *The Plumed Serpent* all bear the marks of hurried composition, of undigested lumps of personal experience, and of journalism. They are novels of travel, of escape from England, and of a search for something beyond the marriage relationship. Lawrence bestowed more care on *Lady Chatterley's Lover* than on any book since *Women in Love*. There are three different published versions (leaving aside the "expurgated" text), and the final version, which we are discussing here, was the result of much labour. The scene is back in the Nottinghamshire-Derbyshire area of the English Midlands, and the theme is largely that of the man-woman relationship.

The story of Connie Chatterley must by now be well-known. She is the daughter of a Royal Academician, and with her sister has grown up in a cosmopolitan world of art and politics. Indeed, we are told that art and politics were Connie's "natural atmosphere," though she shows hardly any interest in either for the rest of the book. During the 1914–18 War she meets and marries Clifford Chatterley, heir to a baronetcy, who "was more upper-class than Connie. Connie was well-to-do intelligentsia, but he was aristocracy."[1] After their honeymoon, he goes back to the War, only to return a few month's later paralysed and impotent. They return to the family seat,

Wragby, a dreary house in the industrial Midlands, yet with grounds and woods still retaining some of the beauty and mystery of the old England of Robin Hood. Clifford becomes a writer and meets with remarkably rapid success. In all that he does, Connie is very close to him in mind, although bodily they are non-existent to one another. It is purely a mental life that they share.

Connie has an affair with one of Clifford's visitors—a successful playwright, Michaelis. This gives her not only a physical, sexual thrill, but also self-assurance and terrific cheerfulness, and these she uses to stimulate Clifford. When the affair ends (after Michaelis has accused her brutally of wanting nothing but her own selfish satisfaction in intercourse), Connie can see little left to live for:

All the great words, it seemed to Connie, were cancelled for her generation: love, joy, happiness, home, mother, father, husband, all these great, dynamic words were half dead now, and dying from day to day. Home was a place you lived in, love was a thing you didn't fool yourself about, joy was a word you applied to a good Charleston, happiness was a term of hypocrisy used to bluff other people, a father was an individual who enjoyed his own existence, a husband was a man you lived with and kept going in spirits. As for sex, the last of the great words, it was just a cocktail term for an excitement that bucked you up for a while, then left you more raggy than ever.[2]

Her husband would no doubt have objected to much of this view, but it is certainly his own as far as sex is concerned. "The casual sex thing is nothing, compared to the long life lived together,"[3] he tells Connie, and suggests that she should have a child by another man.

Connie gets thin and unwell, and her doctor demands a change of scene. She had, so far, herself attended to all her husband's physical needs, but now even this last

contact with him is broken. Her place in his life is taken
more and more by Mrs Bolton, who comes as his nurse.
She is a middle-aged widow who has lived all her life in
the village, and she entertains Clifford with endless tales
of life there. (Lawrence does these wonderfully.) She
supplies a stimulus, where Connie has now failed, and her
stories of the colliers and the collieries turn Clifford's
mind away from his introspective writing towards the
practical problems of reorganising the mines from which
he draws his wealth. Like Gerald Crich in *Women in Love*,
he becomes an astute businessman immersed in the
technicalities of mining—and, like him, too, a victim of
the purely mechanical will.

Connie is left lonely and desolate. Her one solace is to
wander in the woods and, in particular, to the little
clearing where the gamekeeper, Mellors, is rearing the
pheasants. One lovely sunny day the first chick hatches
out. "Connie crouched to watch in a sort of ecstasy. Life,
life! Pure, sparky, fearless new life!"[4] Her one desire now
is to watch the chicks—and there one evening, when
Mellors is present, she breaks down and weeps bitterly at
the sense of her own forlornness. Mellors, moved by com-
passion, takes her and loves her for the first time:

He thought with infinite tenderness of the woman.
Poor forlorn thing, she was nicer than she knew, and
oh! so much too nice for the tough lot she was in
contact with. Poor thing, she too had some of the vul-
nerability of the wild hyacinths, she wasn't all tough
rubber-goods and platinum, like the modern girl. And
they would do her in! As sure as life, they would do her
in, as they do in all naturally tender life. Tender!
Somewhere she was tender, tender with a tenderness
of the growing hyacinths, something that has gone out
of the celluloid women of today. But he would protect
her with his heart for a little while. For a little while,
before the insentient iron world and the Mammon of

mechanized greed did them both in, her as well as him.[5]

Connie and Mellors' subsequent love-making is described with wonderful freshness and tenderness and with a superb command of rhythm that matches both the emotional and physical experience:

She quivered again at the potent inexorable entry inside her, so strange and terrible. It might come with the thrust of a sword in her softly-opened body, and that would be death. She clung in a sudden anguish of terror. But it came with a strange slow thrust of peace, the dark thrust of peace and a ponderous, primordial tenderness, such as made the world in the beginning. And her terror subsided in her breast, her breast dared to be gone in peace, she held nothing. She dared to let go everything, all herself, and be gone in the flood.[6]

Splendidly rendered, too, is the sense of their love being in harmony with the natural world and of the natural world being in sympathy with their love:

As she ran home in the twilight the world seemed a dream; the trees in the park seemed bulging and surging at anchor on a tide, and the heave of the slope to the house was alive.[7]

The best of these descriptions have greater simplicity of language and less sense of strain than anything in the earlier books. And at least one scene has a dramatic power and symbolic quality unrivalled since *Women in Love*. This is the episode where Clifford with Connie sets off through the park in his mechanical wheelchair, which crushes, as it goes, all the wild spring flowers underfoot. On the way, Clifford holds forth about the need to rule the working classes, to treat them as slaves. "Give me a son," he says; he does not care who his father may be as long as the boy can take up his aristocratic rule. Going up a slope, the mechanical chair breaks down, and Mellors, the natural man, is summoned to help. "I know nothing at all about these mechanical things," he says, and offers to push. But Clifford obstinately refuses, insisting that the mechanism must work. Finally, after the chair has completely broken down and Mellors has nearly killed himself trying to right it, he and Connie push it back together. The master has proved impotent, and mechanical will has proved impotent; Connie for the first time "consciously and definitely hated Clifford," and at the same time feels much closer than before to Mellors, who is to be the father of the Chatterley child.

For Connie becomes pregnant. Mellors had given her "an exquisite pleasure and a sense of freedom and life. He had released her warm natural sexual flow."[8] And she wants to marry him. Clifford rages when he at last hears the truth of the affair, and refuses to divorce Connie. But Mellors can get a divorce from his long-separated wife, and then he and Connie will live together on a small farm of their own and have their child. Meanwhile they are apart, and Mellors reflects:

Now is the time to be chaste, it is so good to be chaste, like a river of cool water in my soul. I love the chastity now that it flows between us. It is like fresh water and rain.[9]

The book can obviously be read in many ways. At the simplest level it is in a very old romantic tradition. The aristocratic lady dissatisfied with her husband leaves behind the empty sophistication of the great house to find love in a cottage, in an atmosphere of Arcadian *simplesse* (the homely furniture, the brick floor, the simple fare of beer and cheese and meat). Everything is very clean and neat, of course, and the lover, despite his lowly station, is civilised, sensitive, and intelligent: we remember the shelf of books ("So! He was a reader after all").[10] To the excitement of a clandestine affair is added the delectation of being loved by a man one moment, and addressed as

"Your Ladyship" by him the next. And, in the end, true love wins, and the wicked baronet is thwarted. It is very much a woman's romance, with everything seen from the feminine viewpoint. Thus all the feelings described are the woman's and nearly all the physical description is of the man. Characteristically female, too, is Connie's assurance that she has got the only real man in the whole world:

"Shall I tell you?" she said, looking into his face. "Shall I tell you what you have that other men don't have, and that will make the future? Shall I tell you?"

"Tell me then," he replied.

"It's the courage of your own tenderness, that's what it is: like when you put your hand on my tail and say I've got a pretty tail."[11]

It is natural and proper for Connie to feel that she and Mellors are unique. All lovers feel themselves unique. But upon the romantic talk of the lovers there constantly intrudes Lawrence's moral purpose. When Connie talks about her "pretty tail" she is talking like a woman; when she talks about "making the future" she is talking like Lawrence. (Just as when Mellors, replying to Connie's remarks, says "It's a question of awareness, as Buddha said," he is talking like Lawrence.) We accept the fiction that the lovers feel themselves to be unique. What is unacceptable is Lawrence's implied assumption throughout that they *are* in fact unique—that no other lovers have any tenderness, that no other man tells his woman that she has a pretty tail, that Connie and Mellors are almost the only couple in the country to have a satisfactory sexual relationship, and that they alone will "make the future." The touching romantic story of a man and a woman is always being threatened by the morality in which they lose their humanity and become the paradigm of fulfilment and regeneration in an otherwise sterile and degenerate England.

We are told that Mellors can find no one else to fight with him against the mechanical "Thing"—"the men were all outside there, glorying in the Thing, triumphing or being trodden down in the rush of mechanized greed or of greedy mechanism."[12] But the industrial background of the book, superbly though it is invoked, remains purely a background and not an integral part of the story. Neither Connie nor Mellors has been affected in any way by pressures from this outside world. One cannot see that Connie's problems would be any different if the whole industrial world had been abolished. It is Lawrence (not his story) who constantly makes the point that the world of the mines and mechanism has killed all tenderness between men and women. But, as Lawrence himself said, "Never trust the artist. Trust the tale." And in the tale, the one beautiful example of a fulfilled marriage is that between Mrs Bolton and her husband. He was a miner and they spent their lives in the mining town of Tevershall, which Lawrence describes as the negation of all beauty:

The utter negation of natural beauty, the utter negation of the gladness of life, the utter absence of the instinct for shapely beauty which every bird and beast has, the utter death of the human intuitive faculty was appalling. The stacks of soap in the grocers' shops, the rhubarb and lemons in the greengrocers! the awful hats in the milliners! all went by ugly, ugly, ugly, followed by the plaster-and-gilt horror of the cinema with its wet picture announcements, "A Woman's Love!", and the new big Primitive chapel, primitive enough in its stark brick and big panes of greenish and raspberry glass in the windows. The Wesleyan chapel, higher up, was of blackened brick and stood behind iron railings and blackened shrubs. The Congregational chapel, which thought itself superior, was built of rusticated sandstone and had a steeple, but not a very high one. . . . What could possibly become of such

a people, a people in whom the living intuitive faculty
was dead as nails, and only queer mechanical yells and
uncanny will-power remained ?[13]

Yet this was the scene of Mrs Bolton's warm and tender
marriage. It was also, of course, the Eastwood in which
the young Lawrence and his family and friends had lead a
vivid and civilised life; and the Congregational chapel
was celebrated in his fine essay "Hymns in a Man's Life."

Lawrence included some of his most brilliant polemics
against modern society in this book; the only objection to
them is that they either have no connexion with, or else
(as the case of Mrs Bolton's marriage illustrates) run completely counter to, the story he is telling. There is a
lament for the passing of the old country mansions; yet, if
Sir Clifford's establishment is anything to go by, their
abolition should be welcomed. There is horror expressed
at the thought of "the common people," who are "so
many and really so terrible"; yet with the common
people in the form of Mellors, the future lies.

Here we are back to the idea quoted at the very beginning of this book: "from the middle classes one gets
ideas, and from the common people life itself, warmth."
But, in *Lady Chatterley's Lover*, for the first time, "the
common people" and "life itself" are joined by a third
term, the "four-letter words." These were undoubtedly
the chief reason for the ban on the book, and so much was
said and written about them at the time of the trial that
it would be pleasant to give the subject a rest. But, for
better or worse, they were an essential part of Lawrence's
avowed purpose in the book.

He claimed that "one of the reasons why the common
people keep—or kept—the good *natural glow* of life, just
warm life, longer than educated people," was that they
could use these words "without either a shudder or a
sensation."[14] This is a rather naïve view that would
hardly have survived a day spent in the Forces or in a

factory. For while it is true that these words are used chiefly by the "common people," it is also true that they are used almost entirely as abuse or as expletives or as intensitives, regardless of their original sexual meanings. The way in which they are used is, in fact, the very negation of warm life. Lawrence's intention was to restore these words to their proper use, their original purity. The success or failure of the attempt can be decided only by each individual reader in the light of his own feelings and experience. Thus a man who uses them daily will probably take quite a different view of the experiment from that taken by a girl who has never seen or heard the words before: and the chances are that the man will find them obscene, while the girl may find them innocent and "tender."

Of course, Lawrence's intention was to disinfect the words—to do away with the "dirty little secret," the snigger, the sexy joke. "Pornography is the result of sneaking secrecy,"[15] he said—so away with secrecy. But in doing away with secrecy there lies the danger of violating an even more deeply held conviction of Lawrence's—that sex should be a great mystery, a coming-together in darkness—for how is this to be maintained if everything is to be made explicit and put into words? Here is the ultimate difficulty that faces Lawrence when he wishes to celebrate sexual love: that, in writing about it, he is inevitably having to verbalise and externalise what he believes to be a purely mindless and private thing.

The experiment with the four-letter words causes some havoc in the character of Mellors, the only person to use them. For although he sprang from the common people, he is also an educated man, and for that reason, according to Lawrence's remarks quoted above, should no longer be able to use the words naturally. Thus at one moment he will be talking in dialect liberally sprinkled with these words, and the next he will be saying:

To contemplate the extermination of the human species and the long pause that follows before some other species crops up, it calms you more than anything else. And if we go on in this way, with everybody, intellectuals, artists, government, industrialists, and workers all frantically killing off the last human feeling, the last bit of their intuition, the last healthy instinct; if it goes on in algebraical progression, as it is going on: then ta-tah! to the human species! Goodbye! darling! the serpent swallows itself and leaves a void, considerably messed up, but not hopeless. Very nice! When savage wild dogs bark in Wragby, and savage wild pit-ponies stamp on Tevershall pit-bank! *te deum laudamus!*"[16]

Poor Connie! She has escaped from the cerebral Sir Clifford only to find herself amongst algebraic progressions and Latin tags and the contemplation of extermination in the arms of her lover. But in a minute or two Mellors will turn on the dialect and the four-letter words again. This is the fatal inconsistency in his character. Can one really believe in the integrity of a man who switches at will between two such widely different vocabularies and ways of speech? Connie's sister, Hilda, diagnoses: "He was no simple working man, not he: he was acting! acting!"[17]

The split is due to Mellors being partly a fictional character, but also obviously Lawrence himself in many respects. His father was a miner, but he himself got education; his experiences with his first two girls are exact transcripts of Lawrence's experiences with the Miriam of *Sons and Lovers* and the Helena of *The Trespasser*; and his condemnation of industrial society is Lawrence's own. But while Lawrence's genius, his personal magnetism, and his cosmopolitan wife, made him a classless citizen of the world, Mellors is still in his Midlands cottage, behaving and talking half like a gamekeeper and half like his creator.

Mellors is obviously also a symbolic figure—the preserver of natural life, the bringer of fulfilment to a woman, the adversary of the mechanical world—but, despite this burden that he has to bear in the morality, Lawrence is too much a novelist ever to leave him purely as a symbol. Thus, although he is in one way the preserver of natural life, he himself points out that he is preserving game only for it "to be shot ultimately by fat men after breakfast."[18] On the face of it, Mellors, being partly a symbolic figure, partly Lawrence himself, partly a fictional character, might appear to be hopelessly incoherent. In fact, one must admit that for all the apparent inconsistencies he stays in the mind as a very vivid figure—and one of the few in Lawrence's novels that would pass the old-fashioned test of being immediately recognisable if one met them in real life.

On the other hand Sir Clifford is too much a symbol. By the end of the book he has become a caricature monster, the embodiment of all that Lawrence hated. The case against him is weakened by being overstated. How much more subtle was the presentation of Gerald Crich, who had the same obsession with the mechanical will, yet was vigorously healthy and athletic, who was unsuccessful with women not at the purely physical level, but because of the very mechanical will that had made him a great industrialist. In Gerald the link was made between the industrial life and the personal sexual life that is so obviously missing in *Lady Chatterley's Lover*.

Connie herself is an oddly colourless character, partly perhaps because she has to bear the symbolic weight of being Everywoman. Despite her obvious intelligence, one tends to think of her (as Mellors did) as "just a young female creature." Of the minor characters, the most successful is Mrs Bolton: she is far more than the village gossip, a flat humorous character, because she really does stand for "marriage" in a way that (despite what some of the witnesses at the trial said) Connie and Mellors cannot. She had been "really warmed through" by her husband, who has been killed in a pit accident, and believes that "if there's a heaven above he'll be there, and will lie up against me so I can sleep."[19] As we have seen, when Lawrence uses his novelist's gifts to create a real character and marriage like this, he defeats the moralist in him who has been denying to the mining villagers any rich tender life. On the other hand, Lawrence's attempt to draw a full-blooded, bawdy, old reprobate in Connie's father, Sir Malcolm, is a failure; the conversation between him and his daughter's lover is one of the few places in the whole of Lawrence's work where the tone is disastrously wrong.

Now that the book is at last freely available, it may be hoped that the controversy about its obscenity will die out. Today it seems incredible that such a moral work as Ibsen's *Ghosts* was once vilified as filthy and obscene: tomorrow *Lady Chatterley's Lover* may well be generally accepted as an improving and liberating book. As Bernard Shaw said, "Lady Chatterley should be on the shelves of every college for budding girls. They should be forced to read it on pain of being refused a marriage licence."

Yet the original ban on the book did some good, in so far as it provoked Lawrence to write two essays, "Pornography and Obscenity" and "A Propos of Lady Chatterley's Lover," which contain some of his finest critical and expository writing. They are classic statements of the case for health and sanity against the pornographers on one hand and the "censor-morons" on the other. The case, profound in its psychological insight, brilliant in argument, and based on the history of the last four hundred years, leaves nothing more to be said. One almost wishes that he had written these two essays before the book that provoked them, so that the moral case having been so well stated there would not have intruded, as it does, in the novel.

When Lawrence wrote these essays, so full of life and intelligence, he was already a dying man. For years he had suffered from consumption, but the vivid flame of life inside him had refused to acknowledge the frailty of the body. He was writing almost up to his death, which took place on 2 March, 1930, at Vence, in the South of France. He was only forty-four years old.

REFERENCES

1. *L.C.L.*, p. 10.
2. *L.C.L.*, p. 64.
3. *L.C.L.*, p. 47.
4. *L.C.L.*, p. 118.
5. *L.C.L.*, pp. 123-4.
6. *L.C.L.*, p. 181.
7. *L.C.L.*, p. 185.
8. *L.C.L.*, p. 277.
9. *L.C.L.*, p. 317.
10. *L.C.L.*, p. 222.
11. *L.C.L.*, p. 290.
12. *L.C.L.*, p. 125.
13. *L.C.L.*, p. 158.
14. *L.*, p. 773.
15. *P.*, p. 178.
16. *L.C.L.*, p. 227.
17. *L.C.L.*, p. 255.
18. *L.C.L.*, p. 148.
19. *L.C.L.*, p. 170.

CHAPTER VI

OUTSIDE THE NOVELS

Some account has now been given of Lawrence's ten full-length novels. But these by no means exhaust his fiction, as he also wrote seven short novels, or *nouvelles*, and some fifty short stories. Even so, fiction accounts for little more than half of Lawrence's work. Not only did he write an enormous amount (at least by twentieth-century standards) in the brief twenty years of his career; he also wrote in a variety of forms unrivalled by any other English writer. His poems fill three volumes of the collected edition, and his literary criticism makes a large book; he wrote four travel books, a study of European history, two "philosophical" books, a long essay on education, some plays and many miscellaneous essays. *Phoenix*, which comprises the work still unpublished in book form at the time of his death, contains nearly nine hundred very full pages, and the new edition of his letters is even longer.

Almost as astonishing as the variety of Lawrence's literary activities is the fact that he carried them all on contemporaneously. He did not, like Coleridge, abandon poetry to become a critic and philosopher, nor, like Hardy, give up the novel to devote himself to verse. From the beginning to the end of his career he was always novelist, story-teller, letter-writer, poet, and critic. And the same interests are prominent in each *genre*. For example, Lawrence had a most acute sense of the "spirit of place," but it would be utterly wrong to assume that this was called upon only in the travel books. It plays almost as important a part in the novels and in the stories and poems, while the actual phrase "the spirit of place" is the title of the first chapter of his book of literary criticism, *Studies in Classic American Literature*. Conversely, Lawrence's observation and knowledge of human nature has as essential a place in the travel books as in the novels.

The novels are the central part of Lawrence's achievement, for in them alone are all his powers presented at full stretch. They have, therefore, been given the dominant position in this study. The short stories, though remarkably rich and varied, do not really break new ground. Lawrence's profoundest spiritual explorations are made in the novels; there the man himself is nearly always present in one form or another. In the stories he is not concerned with working out the main problems of his own life, and so is freer to turn his eyes outward to human society and to exercise his acute social observation. This greater impersonality, together with the conciseness of the short-story form, also ensures the absence of the tirades and divagations that sometimes mar the longer fiction.

Social observation almost inevitably involves satire, irony, humour, wit, even cruelty—and these are characteristic features of many of the stories. Many were written about friends and acquaintances of Lawrence (the inquisitive reader will find them identified in Harry T. Moore's biography *The Intelligent Heart*); and, though personal animus may have inspired them initially, it is often transcended in the brilliance of the execution. In other stories, satire is directed not so much against individuals as against types, like the culture-hungry American tourists in "Things." Some of the earlier tales about the "common people" have a quality almost of folk tales: such sketches as "Samson and Delilah," "Fannie and Annie" and "Tickets, Please" show a sort of rough justice being done in a world where not too much is expected of human nature. Sex is often the theme, but sex without the mental complications of the novels. A long-lost husband turns up at his wife's pub and she gets the soldiers billeted there to tie him up and throw him out[1]; a refined girl decides to marry her coarse young man because of, rather than in spite of, the fact that he has got another girl into trouble[2]; a philandering tram inspector is beaten up by the girl conductors he has been playing about with, and told that he must marry one of them.[3] There is no sense of contrivance, of the "well-made story" about these. As in the novels, unconscious forces often motivate the characters. But the stories, being impersonal, nearly all have a definite conclusion, sometimes even a moral, whereas the novels, being the record of Lawrence's spiritual odyssey, always end on a note of uncertainty, looking ahead to the next stage.

The best introduction to Lawrence's shorter fiction is probably "The Captain's Doll." This is a superb long story about a Scottish officer and a German girl, Countess Hannele, set in Germany and Austria after the first World War. The theme is love and marriage, but it is presented in a vein of high comedy. The dialogue, the social background, the whole story is done with an unsurpassed lightness and rightness of touch and yet with depth and seriousness.

The other masterpiece of Lawrence's shorter fiction is "St Mawr." This is very much longer, almost a full-length book, and so it tends away from the classical finish of the shorter tales towards the inconclusiveness of the novels. Its theme, too, turns away from the humanity and civilisation of "The Captain's Doll" to condemnation of much of what we regard as civilised. There are obvious affinities with *Lady Chatterley's Lover*. Rico Carrington is not only a baronet (a most disabling thing in Lawrence); he has also attained the same sort of success in the fashionable artistic world as Sir Clifford Chatterley achieved in the literary world. His American wife, Lou, is vaguely dissatisfied with marriage, and her formidable mother, Mrs Witt, is filled with repugnance for civilised life in general and for Rico and England in particular. The humour of the book is sardonic and grim. On this trio St Mawr impinges. He is a magnificent stallion standing for all that is lacking in Rico and English life. He has independence, "otherness," contact with the deep springs of life. He dominates all the human characters.

Lawrence establishes these characters with remarkable speed and economy and ease, and "St Mawr" is a powerful and impressive story, but a less successful one, I think, than "The Captain's Doll." For here, as in *The Plumed Serpent* and in *Lady Chatterley's Lover*, Lawrence is not only telling a story but also using his characters to expose the bankruptcy of mechanical civilisation and to find an answer to it. His diagnosis of social ills is acute, but the suggested remedies nearly always make a sad anti-climax. In real life, there was Lawrence's rather ludicrous attempt to found a new ideal colony of "Rananim"; in *The Plumed Serpent*, there was the invention of the religion of Quetzalcoatl; in *Lady Chatterley's Lover*, there was Mellors' proposal that all would be well if men wore tight red trousers and carved their stools and embroidered their emblems. In "St Mawr," the splendid horse is shipped off to America, and there quietly abandoned on a dude ranch in Texas, where we last see him ignominiously sniffing round after the owner's mare: the symbol of all Lawrence's positives is come to this! And Lou and Mrs Witt journey on and find a beautiful ranch high in the mountains of New Mexico. So the book ends. We cannot believe that the ranch, wonderfully as it is described, is the answer to Lou's (or her mother's) problems. As an answer it does not impress. But as a piece of travel-writing it is most convincing.

The ranch was, in fact, Lawrence's own ranch in New Mexico, where he wrote the book but, significantly enough, did not stay for long. Lawrence led such a nomadic existence that something must be said of him as a traveller and travel writer. For Lawrence, travel was no luxury but an imperative need, a way of living more intensely. Not only did he move from country to country, from continent to continent; even in one place he was constantly changing his habitation, and the number of houses, cottages, villas and flats that he and Frieda occupied was legion. Vigorously though he reacted to the spirit of place, it could be said that he responded even more vigorously to the spirit of movement. His feelings for a place were never static and permanent (as were Wordsworth's about the Lake District, or Browning's about Italy). And his feelings about people were constantly fluctuating. It was typical that he should write "I loathe and detest the Italians,"[4] and a month later "I am very fond of the Italians."[5] Nearly always the loathing is the result of seeing a people in the mass, while the fondness grows from getting to know individuals.

Going on a journey always brought out the best in Lawrence, and the happiest of his travel books, *Sea and Sardinia*, is nearly all journeying. It is the account of a trip that he and Frieda made in 1921 from Sicily to Sardinia, across to Italy, and back to Sicily. It was a very ordinary trip, such as anyone could take by steamer, bus and train, and they had no adventures. A lesser writer could perhaps rival the description of an impressive natural sight like Mount Etna, but Lawrence's genius shows itself in the transmutation of the very ordinary scenes and people encountered *en route*. The people he sat with in trains and buses, the officials, the guests at the inns, are all touched with a little of his own magic. Their commonplaceness vanishes. So a Sardinian bus-driver becomes half Hamlet, half Mr Rochester, and yet remains a Sardinian bus-driver.

In *Twilight in Italy*, there is less actual travelling, and also less cheerfulness. Most of the book is taken up with a description of life in a village on Lake Garda, where Lawrence spent some time. There is the same convincing evocation of the spirit of the place and the same penetration into the lives of the people, but not the same spontaneous gaiety. Instead there is anger at life becoming mechanised and ugly. The "twilight" of the title is the twilight of the old peasant society, where men ordered their lives by the rhythms of the seasons, worked with their families in their own fields and vineyards, and lived by the fruits of their labours. The young Italians no longer wanted that life. They wanted machines, money, cities, emigration to America. And Lawrence is sick at heart:

I sat on the roof of the lemon-house, with the lake below and the snowy mountain opposite, and looked at the ruins of the old, olive-fuming shores, at all the peace of the ancient world still covered in sunshine, and the past seemed to me so lovely that one must look towards it, backwards, only backwards, where there is peace and beauty and no more dissonance.

Escape from England to Italy had led only to the discovery that Italian peasant life was succumbing to the modern mechanical world as surely as was English country life (as depicted in *The Rainbow*). The same thing was happening throughout the civilised world, so the only further escape is to the past or to the primitive.

Etruscan Places is a journey to the past. Lawrence was fascinated by the Etruscans, that mysterious people living in central Italy, who were destroyed by the Romans, leaving little but their burial places for archaeologists to probe. He saw them as possessing so much of the delicate magic of life that we have lost. But Lawrence was always too much alive to the here and now to lose himself in nostalgic reverie, and the book alternates between re-creation of an ideal past and lively description of raw actuality of twentieth-century Italy.

Mornings in Mexico is a journey to the primitive, for the life Lawrence describes there is far more primitive in many ways than that of the long-vanished Etruscans. The

Mexican Indian has not learned how to use money or measure time and distance. "*Mañana*" may mean to-morrow, three days hence, six months hence, or never. "Two miles are as good as twenty to him, for he goes entirely by his feelings." The book has obvious affinities with *The Plumed Serpent*, and, though it cannot compare with the novel in scope, it has certain advantages over it. For example, the Indian dances described are the real thing, unlike the ceremonials that Lawrence concocted for the followers of Quetzalcoatl, and thus supply a more valid criticism of modern "civilised" life. But however much he wished it otherwise, Lawrence belonged to Europe and to what we call civilisation. He could not stay for long amongst the dead Etruscans or living Indians. What he could do in his writing was to make civilised man more aware of modes of life that he has forgotten—deeper psychic modes (in the novels), more primitive ones (in the travel writings), and the even more elemental modes of animals, birds and plants (in his verse).

Lawrence's poems fall very roughly into three categories—satirical and comic poems, poems about human relationships and emotions, and poems about nature.

The satirical and comic poems are the least important. There is an enormous number of them, mostly very short, little jets of good or bad humour. They have no careful epigrammatic form but the informal air of conversation or of asides in letters. "Talk" is a fair example of the mode:

> I wish people, when you sit near them,
> wouldn't think it necessary to make conversation
> and send thin draughts of words
> blowing down your neck and your ears
> and giving you a cold in your inside.[7]

The second category spells out Lawrence's autobiography again. A glance at some of the titles—"Discord in

Childhood," "Love on the Farm," "Last Words to Miriam," "Last Lesson of the Afternoon"—shows how closely these poems are bound up with the early life and novels. The next stage of Lawrence's experience, the agonies and triumphs of the first years with Frieda, are celebrated in the long sequence entitled "Look! We have Come Through!" Of all these poems about emotional life concerned with Lawrence's mother, early love-affairs, and Frieda, it is generally true to say that the same subjects are treated with more subtley and power in the novels. Poetry is generally held to be a higher and more intense form of art than fiction, but in the case of Lawrence this is not so. His poetry is nearer the naked experience of life (it sometimes reads almost like emotional shorthand notes taken at the time), while in the novels the same feelings or episodes are portrayed in greater depth, having been recollected and brooded over in tranquillity. The poems, in fact, often have more biographical than literary interest.

What distinguishes Lawrence as a poet is the immediacy of his perceptions, and the reason for the comparative failure of his "emotional" poems is that human relations and feelings cannot be immediately apprehended in all their richness and complexity. But the world of nature can be so perceived. And where Lawrence's poetry comes into its own, where it transcends his prose, is in the poems about flowers and animals and birds. He has an instinctive awareness of the "feel," the way of life of an animal, as in these lines from the poem "Kangaroo":

Still she watches with eternal, cocked wistfulness!
How full her eyes are, like the full, fathomless, shining
    eyes of an Australian black-boy
Who has been lost so many centuries on the margins of
    existence!
She watches with insatiable wistfulness.
Untold centuries of watching for something to come,

For a new signal from life, in that silent lost land of
    the South.

Where nothing bites but insects and snakes and the
    sun, small life.
Where no bull roared, no cow ever lowed, no stag
    cried, no leopard screeched, no lion coughed, no
    dog barked.
But all was silent save for parrots occasionally, in the
    haunted blue bush.

Wistfully watching, with wonderful liquid eyes.
And all her weight, all her blood, dripping sack-wise
    down towards the earth's centre,
And the live little-one taking in its paw at the door of
    her belly.

Leap then, and come down on the line that draws to
    the earth's deep, heavy centre.[8]

This is not the greatest kind of poetry, but poetry it certainly is, and of a kind unique in English literature. No
one else has observed animals in quite this way—with
tenderness, penetration and a slangy sort of *camaraderie*—
yet with never a hint of sentimentality. And the form of
the poem is exactly right. What Lawrence wanted to say
could not possibly have been said in the form of a sonnet
or of rhymed quatrains. It could only come in these particular cadences and rhythms and repetitions. In
"Kangaroo" the rhythms suggest both the heaviness and
the delicacy of the creature, and each of Lawrence's
poems about creatures has its own particular speed and
movement appropriate to the subject—"Snake," "The
Mosquito," "Bat," "The Blue Jay," and half-a-dozen
more. There is something childlike about these poems in
the ease and lack of self-consciousness with which Lawrence perceives animals and birds as creatures of flesh and
blood in their own right, with a legitimate place in the

world of their own—not like the idealised Skylarks or Nightingales of the Romantics, or the symbolic Tiger and Lambs of Blake.

Besides these felicitous nature poems, one must mention two moving poems about human life and death— "Bavarian Gentians," and "The Ship of Death," with its impressive opening lines:

> Now it is autumn and the falling fruit
> and the long journey towards oblivion.

> The apples falling like great drops of dew
> to bruise themselves an exit from themselves.

> And it is time to go, to bid farewell

> to one's own self, and find an exit
> from the fallen self.[9]

In both of these poems Lawrence takes a myth, one Greek, one Etruscan, and interprets it in his own way. In each the repetitions give an effect of incantation, yet the flexibility of the verse precludes any sense of monotony. They supply an answer to the criticism of Lawrence as a poet that he lacked craft, that he tossed his poems off without shaping or deepening them. But this charge can certainly be maintained against much of the verse, and Lawrence's own answer was that the lack of finish was intentional.

In the introduction to one of his books of poems, he argued that free verse had its own nature, "that it is neither star nor pearl, but instantaneous like plasm."[10] The classics of poetry are beautiful, perfected, eternal; Lawrence is not trying to rival them, but to do something different—to catch the instant, the immediate, instant self. And he feels that he can do this only in free verse.

But Lawrence still believed that it was a greater thing for him to be a novelist than to be a poet. His essay "Why

the Novel Matters" sets out to do for the novelist what
Shelley's "Defence of Poetry" set out to do for the poet—
to show that he alone is the complete man:

> I, who am man alive, am greater than my soul, or
> spirit, or body, or mind, or consciousness, or anything
> else that is merely a part of me. I am a man, and alive.
> I am man alive, and as long as I can, I intend to go on
> being man alive.
>
> For this reason I am a novelist. And being a novelist,
> I consider myself superior to the saint, the scientist,
> the philosopher, and the poet, who are all great
> masters of different bits of man alive, but never get the
> whole hog.[11]

Lawrence's criticism, like his best poetry, has a
wonderful air of freedom and informality about it. To
him a critic must be a man who is emotionally educated
and "able to *feel* the impact of a work of art in all its
complexity and force." He had no time for "all the
critical twiddle-twaddle about style and form, all this
pseudo-scientific classifying and analysing of books in an
imitation-botanical fashion."[12] Both these quotations
come from an essay on John Galsworthy, and it is typical
that he should have chosen to write on a man whom he
regarded as a comparatively minor contemporary and to
have put some of his most important critical writing into
the essay. Much of Lawrence's criticism is in the form of
reviews, and in this way he dealt with Thomas Mann,
H. G. Wells, Somerset Maugham, and Ernest Heming-
way. But his reviewing was by no means confined to the
novel. Poetry, travel books, memoirs were all treated
with the same acuteness as fiction, and many of his most
important statements come in discussions of books that
are now forgotten.

The reader of Lawrence's criticism will not find formal
essays about the great figures of the past. He never set out
to write directly about any literature earlier than that of

the century into which he was born, although European literature from Homer onwards was present in his mind to be drawn on where necessary to illustrate some point in contemporary work. His one book of literary criticism (with the somewhat forbidding title of *Studies in Classic American Literature*) does not show Lawrence at his best as a critic: it is full of penetrating things, but marred by some of his more strident and repetitive tirades. It seems almost as if he was at his best as an informal critic, when he goes straight to the heart of a book or poem that he is in the process of reading. For this reason, some of his finest criticism occurs in his letters; one striking example is the series of letters about Georgian Poetry to Edward Marsh. In the letters, too, we have his invaluable comments on his own methods and procedures of work, some of which have already been quoted in the discussion of *The Rainbow*.

Not even such a cursory account as this could conclude without some reference to Lawrence's letters. These, written with no thought of publication, give Lawrence a place alongside Keats as the most wonderful letter-writer in the language. Literary criticism, descriptions of travel, polemic, thoughts on art and politics, character sketches of people met—there is infinite variety and veracity to fascinate, stimulate and provoke. In all his work, Lawrence was writing his autobiography, but nowhere did he do so with greater vividness and immediacy than in his letters. Here we come nearest to the flame of life that burned so brightly in the man himself.

REFERENCES

1. *Collected Short Stories*, VOL. II, p. 411.
2. *op. cit.*, p. 458.
3. *op. cit.*, p. 334.
4. *L.*, p. 162.
5. *L.*, p. 169.
6. *Twilight in Italy*, p. 53.
7. *Collected Poems*, VOL. II, p. 239.
8. *Collected Poems*, VOL. II, p. 126.
9. *Collected Poems*, VOL. III, p. 162.
10. *S.L.C.*, p. 88.
11. *S.L.C.*, pp. 104–5.
12. *S.L.C.*, p. 118.

CHAPTER VII

LAWRENCE'S REPUTATION AND CRITICS

In a famous essay written in 1914, Henry James selected the most promising novelists of the younger generation. They were Gilbert Cannan, Hugh Walpole (with *The Duchess of Wrexe*) Compton Mackenzie (with *Carnival* and *Sinister Street*), and last, and decidedly least, the author of *Sons and Lovers*—"however much we may find Mr Lawrence, we confess, hang in the dusty rear." Cannan has long since disappeared below the horizon, Walpole's reputation has declined almost to nothing, and Sir Compton Mackenzie, for all his virtues, is not a major novelist—while Lawrence's planet shines brighter than ever before. Of course, all contemporary attempts to place writers look silly in the light of time: James did not, for example, even mention E. M. Forster, who by 1914 had published all but one of the novels on which his reputation is based. So James's nod in Lawrence's direction deserves credit, all the more so as he must have had to overcome a certain amount of repugnance in order to give even such scanty recognition to a man so radically different from himself in both his life and his art.

This rather grudging praise is the hallmark of nearly all criticism of Lawrence during his lifetime. Some ten years after James's essay, for example, Virginia Woolf in an article "How it strikes a Contemporary," wrote: "Mr Lawrence, of course, has moments of greatness, but hours of something very different." One is reminded of Lawrence's own comment: "They were always telling me I had got genius, as if to console me for not having their own incomparable advantages."[1]

The truth would seem to be that in his lifetime, and for years afterwards, Lawrence's work just was not understood. People *felt* his "genius" or "greatness," but with little comprehension or enjoyment of what he was trying to do. It is astonishing now to read what Dr F. R. Leavis wrote in 1930 of *Sons and Lovers*: "Everyone I have discussed it with agrees with me in finding [it] difficult to get through."[2] This was the verdict of highly educated, intelligent, sensitive people, trained to read literature, on Lawrence's most popular book, which is now read in schools throughout the country: they found it "difficult to get through"! The situation was exactly that described in Wordsworth's classic statement: "Every author as far as he is *great* and at the same time *original*, has had the task of *creating* the taste by which he is to be enjoyed." Usually it is a question of the public coming at last to accept a new form or style of art—as with Hopkins and Eliot, or Monet and Picasso—after bitterly resenting its first appearance. But Lawrence's first books roused no such resentment. He did not do anything shocking with the *form* of his novels; it was their utterly new *spirit* that left his readers baffled.

As we shall see later, Dr Leavis has come to a different and generally higher valuation of Lawrence after re-reading his books over thirty years; and I imagine that anyone who first read them in the nineteen-twenties or early nineteen-thirties and returns to them today will find himself with impressions very different from his original ones. Diana Trilling, for example, writes: "I read Lawrence today and I'm utterly confounded by the effect he had on me and my friends when we first read him: we thought his metaphors were translatable into a programme for practical conduct!"[3] It would seem that the prophetic side of Lawrence loomed larger in 1930 than it does today. The nineteen-twenties saw him as a liberator, an apostle of sexual emancipation, a great figure rather than a great writer—just as Byron had been a century earlier. Moreover his death had the same sort of impact as Byron's. Although no book on Lawrence appeared during his lifetime, no fewer than five were published within a few months of his death in 1930—by Richard Aldington, Middleton Murry, F. R. Leavis, Stephen Potter, and Rebecca West. A year later Murry published a fuller book, *Son of Woman*, "that curious essay in destructive hagiography," as Aldous Huxley called it, "from which you would never suspect [Lawrence] of being an artist. . . . His book is *Hamlet* without the Prince of Denmark—for all its metaphysical subtleties and its Freudian ingenuities, very largely irrelevant."[4] Murry did at least try to deal seriously with Lawrence's work (although from a psychological rather than from a literary angle); but the flood of books that followed was almost entirely devoted to reminiscences of the man. These are even more irrelevant than Murry's book to an understanding of Lawrence's works, but some have real biographical interest—in particular those by Frieda Lawrence herself, by Ada Lawrence (his sister), by "E.T." (Jessie Chambers, the original of Miriam in *Sons and Lovers*), and by Helen Corke (the friend of his Croydon days, who suggested the character of Helena in *The Trespasser*).

The best of the early critical writings on Lawrence was Aldous Huxley's introduction to his edition of *The Letters* (1932). Huxley had been one of Lawrence's most intimate friends in the latter part of his life and the essay is illuminated by this personal knowledge of the man; but he is at pains to insist that Lawrence was above all an artist, and that his gifts were inborn and unaffected essentially by the events of his life (even, for example, by his mother's excessive love). He goes on to define Lawrence's "special and characteristic gift" as:

. . . an extraordinary sensitiveness to what Wordsworth called "unknown modes of being." He was al-

ways intensely aware of the mystery of the world, and
the mystery was always for him a *numen*, divine. Lawrence could never forget, as most of us almost con-
tinuously forget, the dark presence of the otherness
that lies beyond the boundaries of man's conscious
mind. This special sensibility was accompanied by a
prodigious power of rendering the immediately experienced otherness in terms of literary art.[5]

And here "immediately experienced" is a key phrase.
Huxley observes that Lawrence did not approve of the
monumental in art—the symphony or the great building
too consciously elaborated. "He was determined that all
he produced should spring direct from the mysterious,
irrational source of power within him. The conscious
intellect should never be allowed to come and impose,
after the event, its abstract pattern of perfection."[6] This
statement would seem to fit perfectly Lawrence's verse,
and it certainly fits parts of his novels; but it is hard to
believe that such finished works as *Women in Love* or "The
Captain's Doll" sprang direct from this source without
any ordering by the conscious intellect.

Huxley makes too much of Lawrence's concern with
the unknown, with "otherness." This is no doubt where
Lawrence differed most strikingly from Huxley (and
from most other novelists); but to insist upon it does not
do justice to the extraordinary range of his genius. If
Lawrence had written only in this vein, his books would
indeed be hard to "get through"; but even in *The Rainbow*, the novel that comes nearest to Huxley's account—
there are passages (such as the school scenes) remarkable
for their realism. Nor is it true to say that "he refused to
write of the main activities of the contemporary world."[7]
One assumes that Huxley here is thinking of the more
superficial and materialistic activities of life, and not
(say) of sexual relationships. But does not this statement
still make nonsense if one considers, for example, the

detailed picture of bourgeois life in *The Lost Girl*, or the account of the economics of colliery-ownership in *Women in Love*, or the political scenes in *Kangaroo*? Above all, the letters themselves, to which Huxley's essay is an introduction, prove the best corrective to the view that Lawrence was out of touch with the surface realities of people and things.

On the whole, however, Huxley's essay is an extremely favourable and just estimate of the man and his work, but his insistence on the "dark side" probably did Lawrence a disservice in the nineteen-thirties. The world was threatened by forces of Fascism and Nazism; these were dark and irrational; Lawrence was dark and irrational; therefore Lawrence was a Fascist. This was an absurdly mistaken view, but it can be found characteristically stated by Mr John Lehmann, the publicist of the most vocal group of young English writers of the nineteen-thirties:

Lawrence let himself slip more and more into the rôle of prophet of a confused sex-mysticism, an anti-rational cult of the "blood" which at times does not seem to be very distinctly divided from some of the humbugging nonsense of modern fascist theorists.[8]

It is probably true to say that Lawrence's reputation was at its lowest during the War of 1939–45. The latest bibliography does not list a single book written about Lawrence between 1939 (a Swedish book) and 1947 (an Italian book). The controversy that followed his death had died down, and the public had been surfeited with the memoirs of practically everyone who knew him. Moreover, the mood of wartime does not seem to have been very sympathetic to the reading of Lawrence—and there was the purely practical difficulty that many of his books were out of print or hard to obtain.

A change came about in the late nineteen-forties. A new generation had grown up knowing nothing of the nineteen-twenties and not interested in its literary squabbles, a generation which did not have much time either for the refinements of the Bloomsbury Group or for the Marxist-Freudian posings of the writers of the nineteen-thirties—above all, a generation serious and old for its years. The generation of 1918, profoundly disillusioned, saw in Lawrence an iconoclast, a prophet of sexual liberty; the generation of 1945, more serious because it had never had any illusions, saw in Lawrence a positive creative force, the advocate of marriage and fidelity. The nineteen-twenties looked to rationalism and science as the forces that would destroy the fusty hypocrisy of Victorian times and create a new society: the nineteen-forties had all too much reason to fear the power of science, and the search was for some other way (generally outside organised religion) to make a new world.

The two approaches might be symbolised in the persons of Bertrand Russell and D. H. Lawrence. The two men spoke bitterly of one another. To Lawrence, the philosopher was dry, bloodless, sophisticated; to Russell, the novelist was the exponent of a cult of insanity. Lawrence thought of himself as a deeply religious man; Russell has said that he would like every kind of religious belief to die out. Lawrence wanted to make a new world by radically changing men's and women's feelings; Russell sought to make it by improving the machinery of society.

In some ways science and rationalism have triumphed in producing the Welfare State and the Affluent Society, but their very success has made men and women feel more urgently the need for the infinitely richer sort of life that Lawrence offered. The post-war increase of interest in Lawrence is reflected in the reappearance (and considerable sales) of nearly all his work in both hard-cover and paperback editions, and in the publication of a number of new biographical and critical studies. Richard

Aldingtons's biographical *Portrait of a Genius, But. . . .* (1950) was the first reasonably complete account of Lawrence's life, but was soon superseded by Harry T. Moore's *The Intelligent Heart* (1955). Mr Moore is one of a number of Americans who in recent years have shown themselves to be far better biographers of great English writers than their own countrymen have been. An American is probably in a better position to be objective about Lawrence's life—or at least the earlier part of it. An Englishman inevitably sees it from his own class-conscious position in society; he views each of the different milieux in which Lawrence moved—working-class puritan, middle-class teaching, aristocratic intellectual, artistic-bohemian—with his own particular prejudices and sympathies. The danger that faces an outsider to English society is that while he may be impartial he will also be ignorant. Moore, however, went to great pains to soak himself in the background of Lawrence's life and to interview as many as possible of his acquaintances and friends. The result is a meticulous, fully-documented, and admirably balanced account that is likely to remain the definitive biography for many years. However, both Aldington and Moore are concerned with biography, not literary criticism. They differ from the earlier biographers in being both more comprehensive and more balanced.

In the literary criticism of Lawrence, Dr F. R. Leavis's *D. H. Lawrence: Novelist* (1955) stands in a class by itself. As the title suggests, Leavis is concerned with Lawrence only as a writer of fiction, and even here he is very selective in his choice of material for detailed treatment. The short stories and tales take up nearly half the book, and *The Rainbow* and *Women in Love* another third, so there is little space for discussion of the other full-length novels. This balance is, of course, intentional: the emphasis on the two great novels is the essential one in any treatment of Lawrence's work, and Leavis is rightly anxious to rescue the shorter fiction from the neglect in which it has been left. So while he spends only a few sentences on *Sons and Lovers*, he devotes a whole chapter to the short story "The Daughters of the Vicar" (which has obvious connexions both with *Sons and Lovers* and the early part of *The Rainbow*) as a demonstration of where Lawrence's "genius as a creative writer is most undeniable"[9] in the first phase of his career. It is questionable whether Lawrence's genius is more undeniable in "The Daughters of the Vicar" than in *Sons and Lovers*; but it is certainly easier to *demonstrate* that genius from the short story. Here we can see how Leavis's choice of material is partly determined for him by his critical method.

The great difficulty in criticism of the novel is the length of the work under discussion. The reader of a critical examination of a poem can have the whole poem in front of him, or, if it is a very long poem, at least key passages. The student of the drama can read or watch a play in an hour or two and hold it in his mind while it is being discussed. But the reading of a novel as long and full as most of Lawrence's are may take several days, and even the most percipient reader will be unable to retain at the end all the complications of feeling, tone, and plot. But it is Leavis's contention that great fiction demands the same sort of attention and detailed study as poetry— that, in fact, a great novel or short story can be looked upon as a "dramatic poem" and deserves the same treatment. Thus his examination of "The Daughters of the Vicar" is half as long as the story itself. It is obviously impossible to treat all the full-length novels at comparable length.

Leavis was the first person who used the techniques of detailed "practical criticism" on the novel. His starting-point is the actual text, which he often examines down to the detail of a single sentence or a single word. In this way he brings out as nobody else has done the full play of Lawrence's intelligence and art. In particular, his examination of passages of dialogue emphasises the complexity and subtlety of Lawrence's presentation of human relations. Leavis performs one of the most important offices of the critic: he sends us back to his author with an enormously increased awareness of his subtlety and power and makes us see Lawrence and the world he has created with new eyes.

It is significant that Leavis says nothing about the abstraction of Lawrence's "philosophy." He is concerned with the concrete, with human nature dramatically presented. He is anxious to establish Lawrence's "supreme intelligence," normality, and sense of comedy, not only against the detractors who deny him these qualities, but also against the admirers (such as Huxley) who overstress Lawrence's concern with the unknown and "otherness." Chief amongst the detractors, Leavis arraigns Mr T. S. Eliot, who is accused of subscribing "to the general view that, wherever Lawrence's strength might be, it was not, emphatically not in 'intelligence'."[10] Yet Leavis gave currency to something very much like this view in his own earlier book *D. H. Lawrence* (1930), as witness this passage:

> A complete wisdom, it perhaps hardly needs arguing, involves greater concern for intelligence and the finer products of civilisation than Lawrence ever manifests. Against his preoccupation with primitive consciousness and "the old blood-warmth of oneness and togetherness" his concessions to "ideas" and "mind" show as little more than lip-service.[11]

It shows some lack of candour, therefore, when he writes in his later book: "I myself have always felt bound to insist—though it should, I can't help thinking, be obvious—that genius in Lawrence was, among other things, supreme intelligence."[12] One is so grateful for Leavis's second book that one would have no wish to draw attention to what now appear to have been misjudgments in his first, were it not for the fact that he is himself so anxious to parade the misjudgments of Lawrence's other critics over the past forty years. If he chooses to forget completely what he wrote in 1930, it is surely a little unfair that he should also choose to disinter and pour scorn on (for example) an essay that T. S. Eliot wrote in French for a Paris review in 1927.

This sort of cultural sniping is regrettable chiefly because it does not assist one iota in establishing the greatness of Lawrence. How does it help to remark that Tom Brangwen in *The Rainbow* is "so different from any character of Wyndham Lewis"?[13] Of course comparisons with other novelists are important in placing Lawrence's work, but these must be made in some detail to be of any value. Leavis supplies this detail in some illuminating comparisons he makes between Lawrence and George Eliot. But elsewhere what appear to be large claims are made in rather cagey asides, and left at that. For instance, Leavis says that *The Lost Girl* "suggests the work of an unsentimental, more subtle and incomparably more penetrating Dickens."[14] Does this *really* mean that he thinks *The Lost Girl* "more subtle and incomparably more penetrating" than anything that Dickens wrote? If so, the claim surely needs some substantiation. If not, what *does* it mean?

But these points are minor irritants in a critical study which once and for all establishes Lawrence as the great English writer of the first part of this century. Leavis succeeds magnificently in what he set out to do:

> My aim . . . is to win clear recognition for the nature of Lawrence's greatness. Any great creative writer who has not had his due is a power for life wasted. But the insight, the wisdom, the revived and re-educated feeling for health, that Lawrence brings us are what, as our civilisation goes, we desperately need.[15]

To have fallen somewhat under the shadow of Leavis's book was the fate of Mr Graham Hough's *The Dark Sun* which appeared the following year (1956). Hough's book was the first comprehensive study of Lawrence to appear. It methodically discusses all the novels, most of the tales, the poems, the critical and expository works, concluding with a long section on the "doctrine." It covers areas of Lawrence's work that Leavis does not touch. It is a job that needed doing, but it lacks the insight, the discrimination and the passionate concern to see justice done to Lawrence's genius that marks Leavis's book. Hough does not feel Lawrence as a profound "power for life": he sees him as the subject for an academic study. An undergraduate faced with a paper on Lawrence would no doubt find the respectable answers in his book.

A useful survey of the state of Lawrence-studies at the end of the nineteen-fifties is supplied by *A D. H. Lawrence Miscellany*, (ed. Harry T. Moore, 1959; English publication 1961), a collection of some thirty recent essays on Lawrence, chiefly by American writers. Inevitably the standard of these varies greatly, and the weaker essays are object lessons in how not to be a literary critic. Dr Bergler finds that "the effectiveness of 'The Fox' derives from Lawrence's predominantly correct . . . observations of a series of clinically verifiable facts on Lesbianism."[16] To which one can only reply that the effectiveness of this fine story depends on nothing of the kind. Mr Gajdusek goes in for mechanical symbol-counting in *The White Peacock*:

Some 145 different trees, shrubs and plants are introduced; 51 animals are brought in: 40 different birds skim, hover, flit, fly, and wheel through this novel; and many of these function as symbols. There are really few moments in the novel when words are not being used symbolically or with contrived ambiguity.[17]

Nobody would have been more surprised than Lawrence to hear that nearly all the 150,000 odd words in *The White Peacock* are "being used symbolically or with contrived ambiguity." This passion for symbolism affects many of the American contributors to the book. At least half a dozen essays deal with symbolism or myth in Lawrence—mythology being, according to one of the writers concerned, "the most popular literary cult" of our century. But amongst the follies there are some things well worth saying—Mr Alvarez's case for the excellence of the poems; Dr Mudrick's placing of *The Rainbow* not only in English but also in European literature; and Mr Raymond Williams' account of the springs and development of Lawrence's social thinking.

The collection at least is evidence that Lawrence is now being read, discussed and written about more than ever before by critics and academics. But, more importantly, this attention is by no means confined to professionals (as the study of Joyce and Pound largely is). Lawrence is being read by millions of people throughout the English-speaking world, read in paperbacks by ordinary men and women. He may be misread and misunderstood—this happens to all great writers—yet many of these readers will inevitably feel the great influence for life and health that Lawrence wanted his work to have and that he did not live to see. ("I do write because I want folk—English folk—to alter and have more sense.")[18] It is the rage of the artist that he so seldom sees the effect of his work, while all around him he witnesses men of infinitely smaller talents and capacities influencing people and affairs in the great world. Lawrence expressed in *Kangaroo* the bitterness at being cut off, of feeling that one's life's work is making no contribution to mankind. But the men who appeared to be controlling events, the politicians and public figures of those days, are dead or forgotten, and it is Lawrence who is alive and influential, one of the "unacknowledged legislators of the world."

It is not as a "philosopher," or as the prophet of a cult, that he is influential. We can see today that the attempt to extract a coherent doctrine from Lawrence's writing is a futile undertaking. He was the last person to erect any monolithic system. Kate in *The Plumed Serpent* was surely expressing Lawrence's own feelings when she was "weary to death . . . of a god of one fixed purport. Gods should be iridescent like the rainbow in the storm."[19] He was always too much aware of the possibilities of change, of new experiences, always too much alive to them, to be tied to one dogma.

To be *alive*—that was what Lawrence the man was, what his work is, and what he wanted his readers to be. And also to take life seriously—but with a seriousness that is the very opposite of pompous or bloodless solemnity; a seriousness that demands living to the full. The flippant person, the purely sensual person, or the purely idealistic person—these are not "man alive." Man alive is living through all his senses and ideals and aspirations, living with a vital connexion with his own sex and the opposite sex, with birds and beasts and flowers and the whole natural world. It is this life that is presented with such bounty from *The White Peacock* to *Last Poems*; and the lavishness with which it is offered does not involve any lack of discrimination or sureness of touch.

No other English novelist has described such a range of geographical and social backgrounds and captured with so sure an instinct the spirit of each. No other English novelist has penetrated so many varieties of human experience. Not only does Lawrence delve deeply into the feelings which we recognise; he also extends the bounds of our experience by suggesting forms of life hitherto un-realised. All this he does with the art of a great novelist; for, as he said:

Only in the novel are *all* things given full play, or at least, they may be given full play, when we realise that life itself, and not inert safety, is the reason for living. For out of the full play of all things emerges the only thing that is anything, the wholeness of a man, the wholeness of a woman, man alive, and live woman.[20]

REFERENCES

1. *S.L.C.*, p. 3.
2. *D. H. Lawrence*, by F. R. Leavis (1930), p. 8.
3. *A D. H. Lawrence Miscellany*, ed. Harry T. Moore (1961), p. 128.
4. *L.*, p. x.
5. *L.*, pp. xi–xii.
6. *L.*, p. xvii.
7. *L.*, p. xxi.
8. John Lehmann, *New Writing in Europe* (1940), p. 22.
9. F. R. Leavis, *D. H. Lawrence, Novelist* (1955), p. 73.
10. *op. cit.*, p. 23.
11. *D. H. Lawrence*, p. 25.
12. *D. H. Lawrence, Novelist*, p. 309.
13. *op. cit.*, p. 105.
14. *op. cit.*, p. 31.
15. *op. cit.*, p. 15.
16. *A D. H. Lawrence Miscellany*, p. 53.
17. *op. cit.*, p. 194.
18. *L.*, p. 120.
19. *P.S.*, p. 53.
20. *P.*, p. 538.

SELECT
BIBLIOGRAPHY

Note

*In all cases in which two or more editions of any work are
listed, all references in the text are to the edition marked * in
this Bibliography*

I. D. H. LAWRENCE

Ph. = the Phoenix Edition, London (Heinemann) 1954 ff.

1. *Novels*

The White Peacock. New York 1911. London 1911. * Ph., 1955.
The Trespasser. London 1912. * Ph., 1955.
Sons and Lovers. London 1913. New York 1913, 1933. * Ph., 1955.
The Rainbow. London 1915. New York 1915, 1922. * Ph., 1955.
Women in Love. New York (subscribers' edn.) 1920. London 1921.
    * Ph., 1954.
The Lost Girl. London 1920. New York 1921. * Ph., 1955.
Aaron's Rod. New York 1922. London 1922. * Ph., 1954.
Kangaroo. London 1923. New York 1923. * Ph., 1955.
The Boy in the Bush (in collaboration with M. L. Skinner). London
    1924. New York 1924, 1930.
The Plumed Serpent. London 1926. New York 1926, 1951. * Ph., 1955.
Lady Chatterley's Lover. Florence (private edn.) 1928. London (expur-
    gated) 1932. New York (unexpurgated) 1959. * Harmondsworth
    (Penguin; unexpurgated) 1960.

2. *Short Novels and Stories*

The Prussian Officer and Other Stories. London 1914; New York 1916.
England, My England and Other Stories. New York 1922. London 1924.
The Ladybird, The Fox, The Captain's Doll. London 1922. New York
    1923, 1930.
St. Mawr, together with The Princess. London 1925. New York 1925.
The Woman who Rode Away and Other Stories. London 1928. New York
    1928.
The Man who Died. Paris (entitled *The Escaped Cock*) 1929. London
    1931. New York (with *St. Mawr*) 1959.
The Virgin and the Gypsy. Florence 1930. London 1930. New York
    1930.
Love among the Haystacks and Other Pieces. London 1930. New York
    1933.

The Lovely Lady and Other Stories. London 1933.
A Modern Lover. London 1934. New York 1934.
Complete Short Stories of D. H. Lawrence. 3 vols., London 1955.
The Short Novels. 2 vols., London 1955. Vol. I contains "Love among the Haystacks," "The Ladybird," "The Fox," and "The Captain's Doll"; Vol. II contains "St. Mawr," "The Virgin and the Gypsy," and "The Man who Died." Lawrence's other short fiction is all to be found in *Complete Short Stories.*

3. Travel Books

Twilight in Italy. London 1916. New York 1916.
Sea and Sardinia. New York 1921. London 1923.
Mornings in Mexico. London 1927. New York 1927, 1931.
Etruscan Places. London 1932. New York 1957.

4. Poems

Love Poems and Others. London 1913. New York 1913.
Amores. London 1916. New York 1916.
Look! We have come through. London 1917. New York 1918.
New Poems. London 1918. New York 1920.
Bay, a Book of Poems. London 1919.
Birds, Beasts and Flowers. London 1923. New York 1923.
The Collected Poems of D. H. Lawrence. 2 vols., London 1928.
Pansies. London 1929.
Nettles. London 1930.
Last Poems, edd. Richard Aldington and Giuseppe Orioli. Florence 1932. London 1933. New York 1933.
The Complete Poems. 3 vols.,* Ph., 1955.
The Complete Poems, ed. V. de Sola Pinto and Warren Roberts, 2 vols., London 1964.

5. Plays

The Widowing of Mrs Holroyd. New York 1914. London 1914.
Touch and Go. London 1920. New York 1920.
David. London 1926.
A Collier's Friday Night. London 1936.
The Complete Plays of D. H. Lawrence. London 1965.

6. Miscellaneous

Movements in European History (under pseudonym Lawrence H. Davison). London 1921.
Psychoanalysis and the Unconscious. New York 1921. London 1923.
Fantasia of the Unconscious. New York 1922. London 1923.
Studies in Classic American Literature. New York 1923. London 1924.
Reflections on the Death of a Porcupine. Philadelphia 1925.

Pornography and Obscenity. London 1929. New York 1930.

A Propos of Lady Chatterley's Lover. London 1930.

Assorted Articles. London 1930.

Apocalypse. Florence 1931. London 1932. New York 1932.

The Letters of D. H. Lawrence, ed. (with introduction) Aldous Huxley. London 1932. New York 1932.

The Collected Letters of D. H. Lawrence, 2 vols., ed. Harry T. Moore. London 1962.

Phoenix, The Posthumous Papers of D. H. Lawrence, ed. (with introduction) Edward D. MacDonald. London 1936. New York 1936.

Phoenix II, ed. Warren Roberts and Harry T. Moore, London 1968.

Sex, Literature and Censorship, ed. Harry T. Moore, with introduction by Harry T. Moore and H. F. Rubinstein. New York 1953. London 1955.

Selected Literary Criticism, ed. Anthony Beal. London 1956. New York 1956.

II. OTHERS

ALDINGTON, RICHARD: *D. H. Lawrence,* London 1930.

——: *Portrait of a Genius, But . . . ,* London 1950. New York 1950.

ALLEN, WALTER: "Lawrence in Perspective" in *Penguin New Writing 29,* London 1947, pp. 104 ff.

BRETT, DOROTHY: *Lawrence and Brett, A Friendship,* Philadelphia 1933.

BREWSTER, EARL AND ACHSAH: *D. H. Lawrence, Reminiscences and Correspondence,* London 1934.

BYNNER, WITTER: *Journey with Genius, Recollections and Reflections Concerning the D. H. Lawrences,* New York 1951.

CARSWELL, CATHERINE: *The Savage Pilgrimage,* London 1932.

CARTER, FREDERICK: *D. H. Lawrence and the Body Mystical,* London 1932.

CORKE, HELEN: *Lawrence and Apocalypse,* London 1933.

ELIOT, T. S.: *After Strange Gods,* London 1934.

E.T. [JESSIE (CHAMBERS) WOOD]: *D. H. Lawrence, A Personal Record,* London 1933. New York 1936.

GREGORY, HORACE: *Pilgrim of the Apocalypse,* New York 1933. Reissued as *D. H. Lawrence: Pilgrim of the Apocalypse,* New York 1957.

HOUGH, GRAHAM: *The Dark Sun, A Study of D. H. Lawrence,* London 1956. New York 1957.

JARRETT-KERR, W. R.: *see* TIVERTON.

KENMARE, DALLAS: *Fire-Bird, A Study of D. H. Lawrence,* London 1951.

KETTLE, ARNOLD: *An Introduction to the English Novel* (Vol. II), London 1953.

LAWRENCE, ADA (with G. Stuart Gelder): *Young Lorenzo, Early Life of D. H. Lawrence,* Florence 1932.

LAWRENCE, FRIEDA: *Not I, But the Wind*, Santa Fe, New Mexico 1934.

——: *The Memoirs and Correspondence*, ed. E. W. Tedlock. London 1961.

LEAVIS, F. R.: *D. H. Lawrence*, Cambridge 1930.

——: *D. H. Lawrence, Novelist*, London 1955.

LUHAN, MABEL DODGE: *Lorenzo in Taos*, London 1953. New York 1957.

MERRILD, KNULD: *A Poet and Two Painters*, London 1938.

MOORE, HARRY T.: *The Life and Works of D. H. Lawrence*, New York 1951.

—— : *The Intelligent Heart*, New York 1954.

—— (Editor with FREDERICK J. HOFFMAN): *The Achievement of D. H. Lawrence*, Norman, Oklahoma 1953.

—— (Editor): *A D. H. Lawrence Miscellany*, Carbondale, Illinois 1959.

MURRY, J. MIDDLETON: *Son of Women*, London 1931.

——: *Reminiscences of D. H. Lawrence*, London 1953.

NEHLS, EDWARD: *D. H. Lawrence, A Composite Biography* (3 vols.), Madison, Wisconsin 1957, 1958, 1959.

POTTER, STEPHEN: *D. H. Lawrence, A First Study*, London 1930.

SAGAR, KEITH: *The Art of D. H. Lawrence*, Cambridge 1966.

SPILKA, MARK: *The Love Ethic of D. H. Lawrence*, Bloomington, Indiana 1955.

TINDALL, WILLIAM YORK: *D. H. Lawrence and Susan His Cow*, New York 1939.

TIVERTON, FATHER WILLIAM [W. R. JARRETT-KERR]: *D. H. Lawrence and Human Existence*, London 1951. New York 1951.

VIVAS, ELISEO: *D. H. Lawrence: The Failure and the Triumph of Art*, Evanston, Ill. 1960.

WEST, ANTHONY: *D. H. Lawrence*, London 1950.

WEST, REBECCA: *D. H. Lawrence*, London 1930.

WOOD, JESSIE (CHAMBERS): *see* "E.T."

C A P R I C O R N   T I T L E S

C A P R I C O R N   G I A N T S